CLASSROOM SUPERVISION AND INSTRUCTIONAL IMPROVEMENT

Classroom Supervision and Instructional Improvement: A Synergetic Process

by

Jerry J. Bellon
University of Tennessee

Robert E. Eaker
Middle Tennessee State University

James O. Huffman
Middle Tennessee State University

Richard V. Jones, Jr.
Stanislaus State College

KENDALL/HUNT PUBLISHING COMPANY
DUBUQUE, IOWA

Contents

Preface   vii

1. Supervision: Past Practice and New Directions   1
   The Present Dilemma   3
   Recent Influences   4
   New Approaches   6

2. Leadership and Staff Renewal:
   Setting the Stage for Change   11
   Leadership Renewal   11
   Leadership Style   15
   Staff Renewal   16

3. The Synergetic Supervisory Process:
   An Overview   19
   Interpersonal Relationships   19
   Basic Assumptions   20
   Supervision—Observation Phases   21

4. The Pre-Observation Conference   27
   Content of the Conference   28
   Summary   34

5. The Classroom Observation   39
   Observation Limitations   39
   Observation Techniques   40
   Summary   47

6. The Post-Observation Conference   49

Lesson Reconstruction   50
Pattern Identification   51
Pattern Assessment   53
Planning Future Instruction   54
Summary   57

7. The Evaluation Program   59

Assumptions About the Evaluation Program   59
Guidelines for the Development of an
    Evaluation Program   63
Evaluation Instruments   65
Summary   67

8. Improving Instruction: A Shared Responsibility   69

The Supervisor   70
The Building Principal   71
The Department Head   72
The Team Leader   72
Supervisor of Student Teaching   74
Summary   75

Preface

There are many books written about supervision of instruction. We believe that this is one book that should be considered by those who are interested in using the supervisory program to improve instruction. It is not an appropriate book for those who consider supervision an administrative process to rate their teachers.

The concept of synergism is well known in the field of science. It has been defined as the combined healthy action of all elements of a system. We feel that this concept is applicable to instructional improvement. That is, through cooperative action the chances of making and sustaining important changes are greatly enhanced. Keeping this concept in mind we see the supervisory program described in this book as synergetic.

Initially, the basic stages of the classroom supervision process that we present were developed from the Harvard-Newton program. In the early 1960's we were fortunate to hear about this program. Abraham Fischler introduced some of the ideas in a class he was teaching at the University of California, Berkeley. A paper written about the Harvard-Newton program was another source of information. We used the concepts presented in the paper to develop a supervisory process that we could use with the interns we were supervising. The important ideas that we used from the Harvard-Newton program had been generated by Morris Cogan. So, we were strongly influenced by Abraham Fischler and Morris Cogan in our initial attempt at what was called clinical supervision.

For more than ten years we have been attempting to expand and refine our supervisory program as we have worked with school districts throughout the country. Our work in the field has helped us to check our original assumptions and we are satisfied that they provide a sound frame of reference for classroom supervision. However, it has become clear to us that we must address other important problems and issues if our long range goal is to help develop and sustain long term instructional improvement programs.

The leadership style of supervisors and administrators is crucial to the notion of synergism. They must hold assumptions about others in the organization which can be operationalized into cooperative working relationships. Attitudes about renewal are also central to the entire change process. Concerns about evaluation and performance must be dealt with. Out of this complex set of issues, we have had at least one important finding. The processes and procedures used in the supervision-evaluation program must provide opportunities for cooperative, non-hierarchical, working relationships. Power and influence need to be shared by teachers and administrators if development and renewal activities are to succeed.

The material in this book represent our current thinking about classroom supervision and instructional improvement. Because of our concern about leadership development and renewal we have given attention to those concerns. At the end of each chapter we have suggested developmnt and renewal activities which we have used in our classes and in the field. We have found them to be helpful in meeting our objectives. They should also cause the reader to think about and generate other appropriate activities.

We believe that this book should be helpful to any teacher, administrator, or supervisor interested in helping to improve instruction.* We have used the concepts presented here in our graduate level classes in supervision as well as with teachers in general methods classes. We have used the material extensively in our off campus classes and staff development programs.

We do not make the claim that this book or any single book will provide all of the information about the field of supervision. We do hope that those who read this book will find some ideas or approaches which are helpful to them.

J.J.B.
R.E.E.
J.O.H.
R.V.J.

*Note: Throughout the book we have used the terms observer, supervisor, and administrator interchangeably. We know that roles and responsibilities are defined differently depending on school district policy and organizational structure.

Chapter 1

Supervision: Past Practice and New Directions

In order to understand the present dilemma in which the field of supervision finds itself, it is necessary to understand the historical development of supervision. The concept of supervision of educational programs in this country began with the advent of schooling in early America. Communities deemed it appropriate to appoint laymen to carry out the responsibility of inspection, both in regard to teachers and pupils. During the eighteenth century it was common for inspection committees not only to observe the methods of instruction but also to check into their effectiveness by giving examinations to determine the status of pupils' learning. There was little concern about improving instruction by upgrading the teacher. The only remedy for poor instruction was to replace the teacher. It was not until early in the nineteenth century that the powers and duties of the inspection committees were assigned to educational positions. These positions were eventually filled by professional educators and upgrading the skills of teachers became a recognized function. This first stage of the evolvement of the concept of supervision has been called the period of administrative inspection and was predominant until about 1900.

It was during the first quarter of this century that supervision became closely allied with scientific management with a significant emphasis on research and measurement. Supervisors were to discover the best methods and procedures for promoting learning and were to "give" these to the teachers for their use in the classroom. With the emphasis in supervision on inspection and scientific management the supervisor was often seen as a negative person by the teachers with whom he worked. The term "snoopervision" was often used and teachers devised ways to undermine supervisors. They would send signals to each other when a supervisor came in the building and would assign their students to deskwork when the supervisor visited their classrooms.

It seems apparent that supervision was not a cooperative endeavor between the supervisor and teacher and that instructional supervision was

1

not utilizing the principles of good human relations. The negative view of supervision combined with the growing importance of human relations caused the concept of supervision to undergo a series of changes beginning in the 1930's. The authoritarian and punitive attitude that had existed previously began to be replaced with an attitude more in harmony with democratic principles. Supervision came to be perceived as guidance and the emphasis was on working together.

The development of the concept of democratic supervision placed the responsibility on the supervisor to work cooperatively with teachers to help them realize their potential for improved instruction. So, the period of democratic supervision through cooperative group effort saw the supervisor helping to create a conducive atmosphere and environment wherein teachers could develop their capabilities to the fullest extent possible.

While the theories and ideals of democratic supervision appeared to be sound, supervisors had difficulty in applying the principles set forth in the literature. It was difficult for many supervisors to apply the principles of democratic supervision with teachers in the classrooms. Interpretation and application was left largely to the individual supervisor. Many supervisors felt that the best way to operate in a democratic fashion and help teachers realize their potential was to see that they got appropriate textbooks and materials and to otherwise stay out of their way. Consequently, the function of visiting classrooms began to diminish. When supervisors did visit classrooms, they weren't certain about an appropriate procedure to be used, so that many simply observed a lesson without following through with the teacher. In order to avoid the classroom and to avoid threatening teachers, supervisors often occupied themselves with mundane tasks such as delivering textbooks, ordering materials, and completing reports. The supervisor often became an administrative clerk rather than an instructional leader. Supervision succeeded in removing the threat to the teacher but ran the risk of becoming non-functional and non-essential to the educational program.

There were other forces at play which certainly should be recognized. During the post World War II years, schools expanded very rapidly. Many supervisors and administrators were hired who had much of their experience and training in the military. There was a tendency to fall back on supervisory techniques which were more oriented to the military than to schools.

The rapid expansion of schools caused administrators to be overwhelmed with many responsibilities that were maintenance rather than improvement oriented. In the main, school boards did not, or could not, allocate sufficient resources to carry out effective supervisory programs.

As a result of these, as well as other forces, administrators were able to rationalize their lack of involvement in classroom instructional improvement activities.

For supervision to become an important factor in the educational program, supervisors should be able to utilize appropriate human relations processes as well as have the ability to help classroom teachers develop procedures and techniques necessary for instructional improvement. Research conducted during the 1950's concerning the teaching-learning process led to the development of strategies which can aid the instructional supervisor. Several of these strategies have shown a great deal of promise as supervisory aids. They include micro-teaching, interaction analysis, and the use of performance objectives in teaching and supervision.

One of the most promising supervisory approaches is goal oriented. The supervisor works directly with teachers in helping to establish goals for the instructional program and then works with the teachers in moving toward the accomplishment of the goals. This approach is a cooperative endeavor requiring the inclusion of the supervisor in the instructional process.

THE PRESENT DILEMMA

A look at the historical development of supervision indicates that supervision has sometimes been detrimental, sometimes helpful, sometimes useless, but usually maligned. This has brought us to a stage in the development of supervision where it can be said that instructional supervision in the public schools is generally in a confused state. Some agreement exists as to the role and functions of the instructional supervisor in theory; but in actual practice roles and functions are only occasionally and often haphazardly fulfilled.

While the concept of supervision has evolved over the years from that of authoritarian inspection to a democratic-human relations orientation, it is now in a state that may be considered laissez-faire supervision. We mean by this, a confused situation in which a hands-off attitude predominates. Supervisors are so conscious of being seen by teachers as a threat that they retreat from intervening in the instructional process. They avoid direct classroom intervention and therefore have to justify their positions by performing tasks outside the instructional setting however mundane and unrelated to the improvement of instruction these tasks might be. Extensive record-keeping and reporting along with procuring and delivering textbooks and materials have become primary functions of many supervisors. It consumes much, if not most, of their time and energy.

If we are to solve this supervisory dilemma, we must adopt processes of supervision which will allow the supervisor to function effectively. The supervisor should be able to provide dynamic leadership to facilitate the improvement of instruction. We are presently hindered by the lack of a systematic approach to the supervision of instruction. It is mandatory that we develop a system that calls for the direct intervention of the supervisor in the instructional process in a helpful rather than threatening manner. A continuation of the laissez-faire form of supervision can only make the supervisor expendable and leave unfulfilled the essential functions of instructional supervision.

RECENT INFLUENCES

Some recent trends on the educational scene have far reaching implications for the supervision of educational programs. We will deal briefly with only a few of these trends which supervisors must face. Those concerned with the field of supervision cannot afford to procrastinate until emerging trends become established ways of life in the schools. We must plan and project the supervisory operational mode so as to take into account the changes that are upon us. This will place the supervisor in a proactive rather than a reactive role.

One trend which will significantly affect supervision is that of accountability. We are presently experiencing public dissatisfaction with the educational establishment. This dissatisfaction has often manifested itself through the public's reluctance to provide adequate financial resources for the schools. The schools have been hard pressed to show that increased expenditures result in improved learning outcomes. The public, through its legislative bodies, has begun to demand evidence that the schools are achieving the expected results. If such evidence is not forthcoming it is doubtful that increased revenue for operating schools will be made available.

One result of the accountability trend has been performance contracting, whereby private firms have contracted for specific teaching functions in the schools. Another result has been legislation which requires periodic evaluation of school personnel. California and Colorado have passed legislative resolutions which require school systems in those states to develop a plan for evaluation of professional school personnel. Other states are expected to follow suit. Performance contracting and state mandated teacher evaluation are just two examples of recent activities which affect the supervisory function.

It seems probable that supervisors will be called upon to help develop and devise evaluation procedures for professional personnel. It is unfair to hold today's classroom teachers accountable in light of the increasing demands made upon them unless they are provided with proper professional support and assistance. One aspect of the teacher support system is a helpful classroom supervisory program. Any accountability attached to the teaching function must take into consideration the quality and quantity of supervisory and administrative support. Supervisory programs must be aimed at meeting the teaching-learning needs and expectations.

Educators have also heard the cry in recent years for humanizing schools and educational programs. One effort to move in this direction has been the individualization of educational programs. Educators recognize that students have widely differing needs, interests, abilities, and personalities, and there has been considerable effort to develop personalized modes of learning to account for such differences. Supervisors can expect to play an important role in the development and implementation of such programs.

It should be noted that such differences in ability and personality do not exist in students alone, but are often just as pronounced among teachers. While considerable effort has gone into planning individualized and personalized programs for students, very little effort has been expended toward developing individualized and personalized professional support and growth programs for teachers. If we are really committed to the concept of humanization, it will be necessary to develop and operationalize supervisory programs that reflect such a concept. Not only should the supervisory program help teachers develop programs and teaching styles commensurate with a humanistic approach to education, but the supervisory program should also reflect characteristics of humanization. This means that supervisors will view teachers as highly competent professionals who seek assistance for the improved fulfillment of their professional potential. The idea that teachers do not like supervisory intervention must be recognized as an attitude that has been based on poorly conceived supervisory programs.

A staffing trend which is making some headway is that of differentiating roles of school instructional personnel. Differentiated staffing presents new and exciting opportunities to utilize the supervisory concept of collegial supervision. Various teaming arrangements make it possible for teachers to assume different responsibilities. Teachers will find themselves teaching in isolation from other teachers less frequently. This allows teachers to act in a capacity of providing feedback to their fellow-teachers. Such a staffing arrangement also promotes cooperative planning and evaluation of classroom teaching. The teacher will no longer have to wait until a supervisor from the district office pays a visit in order to receive assistance with instructional planning and evaluation. Professional personnel with expertise in instructional supervision can be assigned to specific teams at the building level and may continue in a classroom teaching capacity rather than being removed from the classroom environment to a district office. Such an arrangement should help to alleviate the problem of having so few supervisors assigned to so many teachers.

Accountability and differentiated staffing raise serious questions regarding the tenure system and the graduated salary schedule. The tenure laws were enacted to protect teachers from arbitrary dismissal and to assure an environment conducive to academic freedom. Some groups are now suggesting that such laws protect the incompetent members of the education profession and are calling for their repeal. It is likely that we will see some alternative proposals in regard to tenure.

If the tenure system is altered in the future, we can expect increased emphasis on teacher evaluation. It will become necessary to evaluate teachers and educational personnel throughout their professional careers rather than for the two or three year probationary period in which teachers are now evaluated. Much more sophisticated methods for teacher evaluation must be developed. The long used rating checklist is simply not appropriate.

The supervision program must be prepared to help tackle these problems associated with tenure and teacher evaluation. Supervisors must consider the issues involved in the tenure question and must act positively in encouraging new and improved alternatives to the present tenure system. Supervisors need to work diligently in devising evaluation instruments and procedures that will give some true indication of a teacher's success. When this is accomplished it will be feasible to implement plans for remunerating school personnel on the basis of merit. The development of sound teacher evaluation procedures, along with workable alternatives to the tenure system and effective plans for merit pay are important areas for supervisor and administrator action.

NEW APPROACHES

Much of what is beginning to get attention in current supervisory practice is based upon the utilization of recently developed forms of systematic observation and analysis of instruction. Once those who are serving in supervisory capacities commit themselves to the objective analysis of instruction they will find a number of observational systems available to them. Even better, once the supervisor is familiar with some of the systems he can devise his own adaptations to study those aspects of the instructional process that are of most concern to him and the teachers with whom he works.

One of the best known and most widely used observational category systems is interaction analysis. Ned Flanders (1970) deveolped this system beginning in the late 1950's. The Flanders system assumes that the most vital aspect of what goes on in a classroom is the verbal interaction between teacher and students. Interaction analysis has been used by some supervisors as their total classroom observation system.

Numerous other observational category systems have been developed in recent years. Most of them are similar in nature to interaction analysis. All of them provide a means of observing the instructional process in a rather objective manner. Any of these systems is far superior and much preferable to the often used supervisory behavior of observing instruction from a purely subjective viewpoint, a method replete with instant value judgments and prejudiecd opinions. However, it should be pointed out that any observation system has limitations.

Another development that has been very helpful in the field of supervision is micro-teaching. The techniques of micro-teaching were developed at Stanford in 1963 and are currently in wide use in both pre-service and in-service teacher education programs. Micro-teaching is a system that involves the teaching of a micro-lesson which lasts for a very short time, usually from four to five minutes. The teacher plans a highly delimited lesson and while teaching the lesson concentrates on practicing one or two specific skills. The teacher then analyzes the lesson and often reteaches it to look for improvement in particular skills. Use of the videotape recorder is very popular in micro-teaching, but the system is not limited to videotaping. The teacher who does not have access to videotaping can utilize a skilled supervisor to provide appropriate feedback. Micro-teaching has proven its effectiveness as a system for improving certain specific skills associated with effective instruction.

Programs for appraising instruction have been developed in recent years. George Redfern (1972) has introduced a performance objectives approach to the evaluation of teaching. In Redfern's approach performance criteria are established from which performance objectives or job targets are derived, and performance activities are defined. Performance is then monitored, assessed and dealt with in conference and follow-up activities.

In utilizing the Redfern system, the individual being evaluated must clearly understand what is expected of him. Carefully designed objectives related to day-to-day operational responsibilities and realities must be formulated. This makes it possible for evaluative judgments to be based upon evidence of accomplishment of objectives as well as indications of unfulfilled objectives. An important advantage of the performance objectives approach is that it makes it possible for evaluative judgments to be based on solid information and data rather than on opinions and speculation. If the system is to be effective the monitoring process has to be carefully developed and implemented.

Since the late 1950's, a good deal of work has been done on the development and refinement of a supervisory system called clinical supervision. During this time, Morris Cogan (1973) and associates began working with clinical supervision at Harvard University. A process of experimentation and refinement has been occurring ever since. Clinical supervision is an extremely promising approach to supervision for improving instruction. The system is called "clinical" because it depends upon direct, trained observation of manifest behaviors in the classroom. The supervisor does not deal in generalities but concentrates on specific behaviors that occur in the classroom.

In the clinical process the teacher is not a passive recipient of supervision, but is an active partner whose commitment and participation is essential to the success of the supervisory process. Clinical supervision demands that much more supervisory time than usual is spent with the teacher. A short visit once or twice a year simply will not suffice. If supervision is to be helpful in improving instruction, it requires that considerable time is spent with teachers in the classroom setting.

The synergetic process described in this book includes specific activities which have been derived from clinical supervision. The process includes: a pre-observation conference in which a lesson is discussed and clarified; careful observation of the lesson by a skilled supervisor; and a post-observation conference in which the teacher and supervisor jointly analyze the data and information collected during the observation phase. It is important that specific objectives are determined when planning the lesson. During the observation phase the supervisor concentrates on recording objective data and refrains from making subjective or opinionated judgments. The recorded data then serve as a basis for the joint analysis by the teacher and supervisor of the instruction that took place during the period of observation. This is accomplished during the post-observation conference in which the teacher and supervisor attempt to determine patterns that may have emerged during the instructional process. Identified patterns are then evaluated in relation to the objectives to determine if they enhanced or hindered the achievement of the stated objectives. Future planning of instruction is then based upon the analysis and evaluation.

Synergetic supervision emphasizes human relations in the supervisory process. Those who work with clinical supervision also recognize that good human relations are essential to the success of the clinical process. The supervisor should spend considerable time developing good relations with teachers before visiting their classrooms for the purpose of observation. It is suggested that summer workshops and in-service programs be devoted to explaining and demonstrating the clinical process to teachers who will be involved. This also gives the supervisor an opportunity to develop some comfortable relationships with the teachers. It should be emphasized, however, that no matter how much effort is expended to build trust and positive relations between supervisor and teacher the teacher is likely to be somewhat uneasy in the initial stages of the clinical process. Probably the best way to build real trust between the teacher and supervisor is to carry out the entire supervisory process. Once the teacher has been through the process and understands what the supervisor is attempting to do a trusting relationship is likely to ensue.

One valuable carry-over of the synergetic supervisory program is to cause teachers to look at their instruction analytically. Once teachers learn and develop expertise and skill in the methods and procedures utilized in synergetic supervision they will find themselves in a position to help each other analyze instructional behavior and will be able to analytically assess their own instructional behavior.

The major purpose of the synergetic process is the development and renewal of teachers and administrators so that the instructional program can be improved. The ultimate goal of the synergetic process is instructional change and improvement through the collective efforts of teachers, supervisors and administrators.

REFERENCES

1. Allen W. Dwight and David B. Young. "Television Recording: A New Dimension in Teacher Education." Unpublished Paper, Stanford University, School of Education.
2. Cogan, Morris L. *Clinical Supervision.* Boston: Houghton Mifflin, 1973.
3. Flanders, Ned A. *Analyzing Teaching Behavior.* Reading, Mass.: Addison-Wesley Publishing Co., 1970.
4. Lucio, William H. and John D. McNeil. Supervision: *A Synthesis of Thought and Action.* New York: McGraw-Hill, 1969.
5. Redfern, George B. *How to Evaluate Teaching Performance.* Worthington, Ohio: School Management Institute, 1972.

DEVELOPMENT AND RENEWAL ACTIVITIES

1. To better understand the historical development of supervision read the first twenty pages of Lucio and McNeil.

2. A concise review of the state of supervision is presented in the ASCD publication *Supervision in A New Key*. A careful reading of this booklet would be most helpful to anyone interested in understanding current supervisory approaches.
3. For those interested in a carefully detailed description of clinical supervision, Cogan's book is highly recommended.

Chapter 2

Leadership and Staff Renewal: Setting the Stage for Change

While many new instructional approaches are tried in the schools these days, too often, there is a lack of success in sustaining even the most promising innovation. Studies have suggested that the single most important factor in any major educational change is the presence of a strong leader who is committed to the new approach. This chapter focuses on the attitudes, skills, and competencies needed by the instructional leader and staff necessary to begin a synergetic supervision process.

LEADERSHIP RENEWAL

The supervisor, principal, or other organizational leader, who is committed to organizational change must also have a personal philosophy oriented to self-renewal. If the individual is not a self-renewing person, there is little hope for organizational renewal. There are several ways to look at renewal. John Gardner (1965) has examined the concept in considerable detail. Renewal as Gardner views it is a process not only aimed at new ways of doing things but also new ways of thinking. Further, an individual does not remain in steady state but will either progress or regress. The self-renewing individual will help keep the organization from deteriorating or remaining in steady state.

Much has been said about leaders having risen to a level of incompetence. It is true that many good teachers would not be good administrators or supervisors, and that good building administrators have failed in central office assignments. Because people fail, it is easy to say that they are incompetent. We take the position, however, that people fail, not because they lack ability, but because they are not using their best or most appropriate abilities. Too often the leader is using much of his energy to maintain his position and his status. The chance of success is greater when the leader is using his energy to develop himself as a self-renewing person.

11

Attitude Renewal

Perhaps the most difficult, as well as the most important, type of renewal is that which deals with attitudes. It is somewhat easier to learn new things or even new skills, but developing new attitudes requires a real sense of purpose. Gardner has pointed out that a person must have motivation, commitment, and conviction in order to be a self-renewing individual. These intangibles add up to a frame of reference about self-renewal which is largely attitudinal. Supervisors and teachers must believe that they can improve and become something more than they are. When this belief becomes a part of organizational life, more educators will increase their personal satisfactions and professional competencies.

An initial step in developing an attitude toward personal self-renewal is to become more aware about ourselves as individuals. We need to know how others perceive us as well as how accurate our own self-perceptions are. What do we really know about ourselves and what do others know about us? One frame of reference about self-awareness has been developed by Joseph Luft (1970). He has conceptualized the Johari Window—an effort to depict what an individual knows about himself and what others know about him. Although the Johari Window concept has not met with universal acceptance it does present a way of looking at oneself. It also can be used as an aid to analyze group interaction.

The instructional leader must analyze the feedback that comes from those with whom he is working. The leader has the responsibility to clarify his attitudes to others and accept the attitudes that others are attempting to communicate. The instructional leader may find that a review of the principles in the Johari concept will aid in attitude self-assessment.

Productive relationships are based on clear communication patterns. You must want to hear and listen to people if you are going to communicate effectively. Your ability to communicate clearly to others is based on your attitude about yourself and about those with whom you are in contact. Positive two-way interpersonal communication is basic to improved self-awareness and to personal attitude clarification. However, positive two-way communication is often difficult to achieve in an organizational setting. It is incumbent upon the leaders in an organization to develop positive attitudes about those with whom they work. Without this attitude from the leaders it may well be impossible to develop positive attitudes among and with the subordinates. If positive attitudes are not developed there is little possibility that there will be clear communication in the organization. Suspicion tends to increase and motives are often questioned. Conversely, where positive relationships have been developed, communication tend to be clear and better interpersonal relationships exist.

Positive interpersonal communication then is critical to organizational health and renewal. It is a process which requires a maximum level of self-awareness as well as accurate perceptions about relationships with others. Sometimes it is a painful process but it is essential if trusting and facilitating relationships are to exist in organizatons.

Skill Renewal

It is not only necessary to have an attitude which supports change, but it is also often necessary for the leader to improve or develop interpersonal skills. For example, increasing one's awareness of the needs of others requires effective listening skills. One method widely used to improve listening skills is to practice "paraphrasing."

Paraphrasing is the process of clarifying, extending or restating a statement prior to communicating a response. This skill is used regularly by the supervisor who is attempting to clarify a teacher's instructional intent. For example, the teacher may say that he will be teaching the causes of the Civil War. Through the paraphrasing process the supervisor may help the teacher become more specific about expected learning outcomes as a result of the instruction. In this situation, the paraphrasing technique is used to restate the general or nebulous idea to a more specific set of objectives.

Paraphrasing (also called active listening) provides an effective way to communicate to the teacher a real feeling of interest in what the teacher is attempting to do. Once this interest has been conveyed, the working relationship between the supervisor and the teacher is likely to be more open and positive toward the supervisor.

Another communication skill which can be very helpful to the supervisor is the process of differentiating between behavior descriptions and feelings descriptions. As one works with teachers and visits classrooms, it is important to be able to differentiate between describing what is seen and what one feels about what is observed. A behavior description is an attempt to verbalize the actual facts of a situation. A feelings description, however, is the process of verbalizing one's feeling's attitudes, or assessment of a situation.

The skills of describing behavior and feeling may be practiced in group meetings by discussing the topic and then asking group members to try differentiating their statements into these two categories. The effective supervisor can quickly establish the importance of clear and useful feedback through these rather simple processes.

Supervisors work with groups of people as well as with individuals. There are several skills which can facilitate group meetings. For example, the group leader must be skilled in identifying the different roles that members of the group are fulfilling. It is important to be able to identify those who are attempting to block all the good ideas of a group. It is also important to know which members of a group are promoting the activities of a group. There are various group roles that are played out in such a situation. The leader of the group must be skilled at identifying these roles and determining the effect that they have on the operation of the group.

Douglas McGregor (1960) has spelled out those characteristics which indicate productive groups as opposed to the characteristics of non-productive groups. These characteristics constitute a good frame of reference to use in analyzing group effectiveness. A skillful leader would be able to identify the kinds of characteristics that are being exhibited by the groups which are working with him. This process can be most helpful in determining ways to improve group productivity.

Knowledge Renewal

In addition to having an attitude which encourages renewal and skills necessary for productive change, there is, of course, the need to know about current developments in curriculum and instructional theory. For example, during the past decade considerable attention has been given to curriculum and program development. There have been new models, sometimes very complex, that deal with curriculum development. The instructional leader or supervisor needs to know about these changes and be able to identify the developments in curriculum planning which will be most beneficial to his own school and school system. It is inappropriate for the instructional leader to be dealing with curriculum development theories and assumptions which are not congruent with the needs of his clientele.

The behavioral objectives movement, for example, has caused a decided shift of emphasis in terms of learning and the learner. The instructional leader is placed in the position of having to make decisions about the use of behavioral objectives and the emphasis on specifying learning objectives.

Renewed attention to evaluating learning outcomes has several implications. The value of pre-assessing the learner or determining his entry level abilities is being emphasized. This is an essential process if one is to individualize instruction. Teachers are also expected to expand their view of student evaluation. The use of criterion-referenced instruments has increased considerably as more attempts are made to individualize instruction. As various evaluation techniques continue to be refined, it will be important for the instructional leader to become fully aware of developments in this field.

The classroom teachers are going to need more and more guidance in the use of mediated instruction. While the use of media has been relegated too often to overhead projectors and 16mm projectors, the current trend is toward mediating instruction with a variety of equipment and materials. Teachers and supervisors will be involved in instructional improvement of activities which include greater attention to processes for mediating instruction.

These examples suggest that the instructional leader faces a real challenge if the demands of the organization and the needs of teachers and students are to be met. The systematic renewal of attitudes, skills, and knowledge must be a high priority for those in leadership positions.

LEADERSHIP STYLE

The leadership style of the supervisor is very important to the synergetic process. Discussion about leadership style has often focused on the advantages of the democratic approach as opposed to the autocratic approach to administration.

Current thinking about leadership emphasizes situational leadership. Situational leadership can be thought of as the process which emphasizes the situation as well as the leadership philosophy. Therefore, certain crisis types of situations may require rapid unilateral decisions. On the other hand, decisions which are going to influence many people over a longer period of time may require a high level of involvement by those affected by the decisions.

Doublas McGregor (1960) has developed two theories which may reflect most leadership styles. Theory X is based on a set of assumptions which indicate that people need to be directed and controlled because they do not like to work. Theory Y is based on the assumptions that creativity is widely spread throughout the population, that human beings are motivated, and that people do not need to be directed and controlled.

An individual's leadership style is a reflection of these assumptions. The person who holds largely Theory X assumptions will be more likely to direct and control the subordinates. The person holding Theory Y assumptions will tend to involve subordinates in the decision-making process.

Tannenbaum (1973) has developed a continuum of leadership behavior which helps depict situational leadership. This model suggests that a leader may use different decision-making modes depending on the situation. For example, leaders may tell people what to do, sell them on an idea, or involve them in the decision-making process. We would contend that a person may hold Theory Y assumptions and, at the same time, a situation may arise which requires a unilateral decision. This does not mean that the leader has changed his assumptions about others in the organization, but instead that the situation has changed.

The leadership style which is developed by a supervisor needs to be carefully assessed in terms of the goals of his organization and the expectations of his position. If the supervisor has increased his self-awareness and is getting adequate feedback about what he is doing, he will be in a position to determine how well his style is matching up with the organizational goals. It is important for the supervisor to develop a style which is congruent with his own personality and which will permit the other members of the organization to work in a cooperative fashion. If the leadership style is based entirely on the Theory X assumptions, there is very little possibility that cooperative relationships will be developed.

STAFF RENEWAL

Personal self-renewal is the first step toward total staff renewal. A leader who has become a self-renewing person is in a position to help others on the staff become renewal oriented. In order to move a teaching staff toward the synergetic process a plan for change is needed. Basic to this plan is the understanding by the staff that the leader is well-prepared and that he is competent.

This competency can be communicated to the staff in a number of ways. For example, the leader must show the staff that he is well acquainted with current instructional and curriculum trends. He must be in a position to discuss these trends and developments with the staff. He would also be in a position to conduct inservice programs which focus on current instructional approaches. The leader should help the staff plan and evaluate any new curricular ideas. He will need to help establish goals and objectives for change. The key to effective change is the ability of the leader to involve others in the development of new programs and processes.

Once a decision is made to implement a new supervisory approach, it is essential that the entire program be planned in great detail. The planning must include a careful delineation of the goals and expectations. Provisions for feedback and evaluation on a regular basis must be specified. The supervision program will need to be adjusted to meet the individual needs of building personnel and central office staff. In order to be successful, a systematic plan is needed which allows for flexibility and at the same time gives a sense of direction and purpose to all concerned. When the staff has discussed and examined the approach and a plan has been developed, the supervisor may then begin to work with individual teachers.

Both the synergetic process of supervision and the performance objectives approach to teacher evaluation present means by which the supervisor and teacher can jointly and cooperatively evaluate and assess instructional success on a more objective basis. Such supervisory and evaluative methods move us in the direction of solving the teaching evaluation dilemma and present important opportunities for improving the teaching function.

While improved supervision is helpful in developing analytical approaches to assessing and improving teaching, a primary goal must be to encourage and prepare teachers to view their own and each other's teaching objectively and from a clinical point of view. Once teachers adopt an analytical approach to viewing their own teaching it is necessary that they acquire appropriate skills related to the analysis of teaching in order that they be able to evaluate and improve their own performance. This casts supervision into a teaching medium so that supervisors can assist teachers in acquiring the skills necessary for viewing instruction analytically. The supervisor should help prepare teachers in forms of self-supervision. Once teachers possess the skills necessary for good supervision they will be in a position to evaluate their own instruction.

Inservice training efforts should be directed at training teachers to function in supervisory and evaluative roles. When teachers are able to function interchangeably in the roles of teacher and supervisor, it will no longer be necessary to await the arrival of an external staff member to perform supervisory functions. The dilemma of not having enough supervisory personnel to provide an effective observation-evaluation program will be partially solved.

Staff renewal through inservice education activities can be very effective when all of the personnel are working toward developing an improved process. Effective leadership, positive attitudes, good planning, and common goals are all essential to productive staff renewal programs.

REFERENCES

1. Gardner, John W. *Self Renewal: The Individual and the Innovative Society.* New York: Harper and Row, 1965.
2. Luft, Joseph. *Group Processes: An Introduction to Group Dynamics.* Palo Alto, California: National Press Books, 1970.
3. McGregor, Douglas. *The Human Side of Enterprise.* New York: McGraw-Hill, 1960.
4. Tannenbaum, Robert and Warren H. Schmidt. "How to Choose a Leadership Pattern." *Harvard Business Review,* May-June, 1973, pp. 162-180.

DEVELOPMENT AND RENEWAL ACTIVITIES

1. To analyze your own leadership pattern review the Tannenbaum model and compare to your decision-making behavior.
2. For a better understanding of your leadership style read McGregor's Theory X and Theory Y assumptions and compare them to your assumptions about others.
3. Another form of leadership assessment is to ask those with whom you work to give you feedback about the assumptions you exhibit in the leadership role.
4. *Up the Organization* by Townsend is a popular paperback which is enjoyable to read yet helpful in reflecting on one's own leadership style.
5. If you are interested in developing a plan for personal self-renewal, begin by reading Gardner's book. It is short, easy to read, and highly stimulating.
6. Interpersonal relations in an organization can be improved. Begin by making a list of everyone with whom you work. Note those with whom you have either a plus or minus relationship. Develop a plan to begin to convert those which are minus to plus relationships.

Chapter 3

The Synergetic Supervisory Process: An Overview

A description of the total synergetic process is necessary to show how various elements fit into the entire system. This chapter is devoted to a brief presentation of the activities and assumptions which are basic to the development of a synergetic system. Detailed discussions about each process phase are presented in the following chapters.

INTERPERSONAL RELATIONSHIPS

Both the leader and the staff need to be well prepared to initiate and sustain important instructional changes. This preparation includes a commitment to new ideas and improved practice. Commitment and motivation are necessary but not enough. A willingness to develop new skills and gain new understandings is essential to improved practice.

Improved supervisor-teacher relationships are one goal of the synergetic process. Much is said about developing positive and trusting relationships. Positive interpersonal relationships are most helpful when a group begins to work on new approaches to instructional improvement.

We believe that good communication is based on positive feelings in a group. We refer to this as a plus-plus condition. If part of the group is positive and others are negative, communication will be impaired. This is referred to as a plus-minus condition. When all members of a group have negative feelings, a minus-minus condition exists, there is little communication and a great deal of hostility. Lundstedt (1969) sees the development of positive relationships as a key factor in improving communication.

Improved self-awareness and certain skill sessions can help in developing plus-plus relationships. This development should be done prior to initiating new programs. But once a program is started, the processes inherent in the program should reinforce and extend the plus-plus condition.

The synergetic process of supervision is aimed at building more productive and positive attitudes. Each activity and process is based on improving competencies of the supervisor and the teacher. The final and most important outcome is a more productive environment for the learners.

BASIC ASSUMPTIONS

Inherent in the development of any program is a specific set of assumptions. The assumptions listed in the following materials are those which preceded the development of the synergetic process for improving instruction.

Assumption 1

Teaching is a set of identifiable patterns of behavior. We believe the research on human behavior supports the contention that human behavior can be categorized, and that teaching is one specialized group of human behaviors. Further, we would support the notion that as a category of human behavior, teaching behavior itself can be observed, categorized, analyzed, and changed. This assumption deals with the long standing discussion about whether or not teaching is purely an art. There are those who believe good teachers are born and not made. If one were to take this position there would be very little need for instructional supervision.

We take the position that certainly some teachers seem to be more artistic than others. However, even the most artistic teacher can improve. There are well over two million teachers in classrooms in this country. Most, if not all, of these teachers want to improve and can improve. Together the teachers and the supervisors can identify patterns of teaching behavior which are central to the instructional process.

Assumption 2

When selected patterns of teaching behavior are changed, improvement of instruction can be achieved. Much research in education is presently directed toward the critical analysis of the teaching act. Whereas some researchers have defined specific behaviors as essential to effective teaching, many have described certain behaviors only associated with effective learning. Further, the position taken in this system is that any significant change in the complex of teaching behaviors will more likely occur if specific behaviors are isolated for study. In this manner, the teacher can focus on one element in his teaching, rather than on the whole set of behaviors.

The element to receive attention becomes identified as a teaching pattern. A pattern is considered to be any behavior which is regularly repeated. When specific patterns are identified and then related to the teacher's objectives, a decision can be made about changing those which do not support the objectives. Through this process instruction can be improved.

Assumption 3

The supervisor-teacher relationship must be built on mutual trust if change is to take place. If a teacher is going to make certain behavior changes, an awareness about the need for change must be established. It is axiomatic that threat tends to decrease awareness while trust tends to increase awareness. Therefore, we assert that a strong, positive relationship must exist between the teacher and the supervisor in order to bring about instructional improvement.

We would hope that the supervisor-teacher relationship begins with a trust or plus-plus relationship. If the relationship is to continue to be positive there must be continued cooperative improvement activities. The trust relationship can be continued and extended through the synergetic process. It comes from a doing or active interaction rather than from just talking or verbalizing about the need for trust.

Assumption 4

The improvement of instruction is the primary goal of supervision. As a supervision process, synergetic supervision is designed to provide a vehicle for the improvement of instruction. Systems designed primarily to evaluate people or processes, unless the evaluation is limited to self-evaluation, have been all too typical of educational supervision in the past. This program emphasizes teacher-supervisor interaction in order to more effectively and efficiently achieve predetermined educational objectives. The evaluation of this interaction is a spin-off of the process and is secondary to the primary purpose of instructional improvement.

SUPERVISION—OBSERVATION PHASES

The instructional supervision component of the synergetic system is composed of three highly interrelated phases. A fourth phase which is partially an outcome of the first three is the evaluation program. The relationship and elements of the four phases are depicted in Figure 1. A brief discussion of each phase is presented below.

Phase 1

Pre-observation conference. During this phase of the process the supervisor has an opportunity to build on the previously established trust

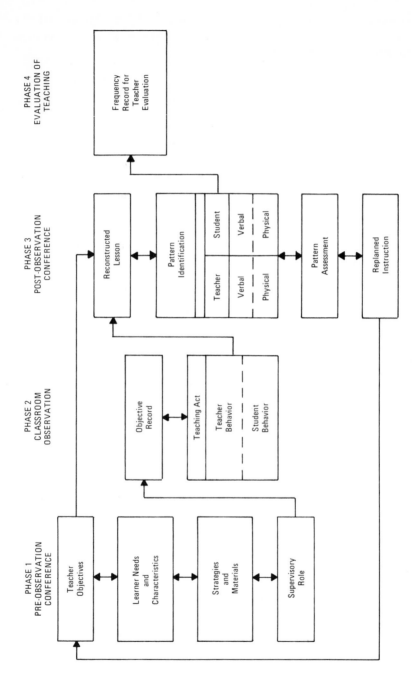

Figure 1. Schematic representation of the supervisory process.

relationship. The role of the supervisor should be explained and the processes to be used should be clarified. The steps in the pre-observation conference are summarized below.

a. Discuss the class setting. The teacher should help the supervisor understand the nature of the lesson to be observed, its relationship to the larger area of study, and how the entire area fits into the total curriculum.

b. Clarifying objectives. The objectives for the class should be specified by the teacher in terms of *learner* outcomes. These may be both content and process objectives.

c. Learner characteristics and evaluation. The readiness of the learner needs to be discussed. In addition the pre and post assessment processes should be described.

d. Strategies and materials to be used. The teacher should describe the teaching strategies (methods) to be employed as well as any materials needed to conduct the class.

e. Establishing the supervisory role. Based on the objectives of the class and the strategies to be employed the teacher and supervisor should agree on a focus that will be most helpful to the teacher.

Phase 2

Classroom observation. During this phase, the classroom behavior of the teacher and the students is observed and recorded. It is not possible to record everything that is taking place. Therefore, the observer (whether supervisor, principal, or fellow teacher) and the teacher decide on selected behaviors to be observed during the pre-observation conference. For example, attention may be given to the verbal or physical behavior of the students or of the teacher. Another alternative is to observe and record a combination of teacher and student behaviors. It must be emphasized that the observer is to record only that behavior which can be observed. Value judgments must not be a part of the record.

Phase 3

Post-observation conference. This conference is the most critical phase of the program. This is where important face-to-face discussions take place. The supervisor or observer who has worked to master plus-plus interpersonal relationships will find this phase to be highly productive.

The first task in the conference is to share with the teacher what has been recorded. Mutual attention to recorded data can help focus on teaching. In order to systematically analyze the recorded data the following steps are recommended.

  a. Reconstruct what took place. The teacher and the supervisor should go over the data and come to an agreement as to the accuracy of the record. This agreement must be reached before proceeding.
  b. Identify behavior patterns from the recorded data. A pattern may be any action which seems to recur. It may be physical or verbal. It may be a teacher pattern, a student pattern, or a combination of the two.
  c. Re-state the process and content objectives for the lesson from the pre-observation conference.
  d. Compare the patterns which have been identified with the stated objectives. Determine the congruency of the patterns and the objectives. Together, assess the relationship of the patterns to the objectives. It is important to note that the patterns have little inherent value unless they are analyzed in terms of the teacher's objectives.
  e. Use the analysis to plan future teaching. The supervisor and the teacher should agree on those patterns which have supported the teacher's objectives. Continued use of these patterns would be recommended. There should also be agreement as to which patterns need to be changed or modified. An attempt should be made to plan an instructional activity which may lend itself to changing or strengthening certain patterns.

The steps recommended for the post-observation conference have been found to be successful in developing an attitude which facilitates instructional change and improvement. Supervisors have often found that it takes a great deal of effort to change their own behavior in order to conduct a successful conference.

Phase 4

Evaluation program. The data gathered during the observation and discussed in the post-observation conference will be important for that component of the evaluation program which deals with teaching. The evaluation program should be based on the assumption that the major purpose of evaluation is to gather information for decision-making which will improve the instructional program. If negative aspects of evaluation dominate the thinking of teachers and supervisors, very little can be gained from the information collected during the supervisory process.

All aspects of the evaluation program should be in harmony with supervisory procedures. Agreement needs to be reached about the important behaviors which will be evaluated and given close attention by all concerned with the instructional program. The evaluation forms need to be congruent with the procedures used to gather data for evaluation decision-making. Rating sheets heavily laden with value statements which require subjective value judgments would not be effective in the synergetic process.

Finally, each school district needs to build its own evaluation program. The unique characteristics of a school district should be given careful consideration as the evaluation program is developed.

REFERENCES

1. Lundstedt, Sven. "Conflict Management: Preeminent Challenge in Administration." *Bulletin of Business Research*, January, 1969. pp. 1-9.

DEVELOPMENT AND RENEWAL ACTIVITIES

1. Identify the phases of the supervisory process in a school district and compare to the phases in the Synergetic Process.
2. Review other supervisory programs described in the literature and identify the important phases in those programs.
3. From an analysis of this chapter and activities 1 and 2, determine which supervisory areas you feel need the most attention to improve instruction in a given school or district.

Chapter 4

The Pre-Observation Conference

Prior to the actual classroom observation, the supervisor should always meet with the teacher for a pre-observation conference. In the pre-observation conference the supervisor will need to use all of the human relations and skills at his command. Although there are definite points to be covered in the conference, the feeling that a teacher has as a result of talking and working with the supervisor determines, to a great extent, if the teacher will attempt to improve classroom behavior. Thus, the long term goal of any conference between the supervisor and teacher should be the development of an open and honest relationship.

Ideally, some explanation or training in the supervisory process should have been made available to the teacher prior to the conference. Whether this was done or not, the supervisor should briefly review the supervisory process. In describing the process every effort should be made to assure the teacher that the purpose of a classroom observation is not to reform the teacher's personality or style. The focus of the observation will be upon the behaviors exhibited in the classroom.

The dynamics of the pre-observation conference will depend largely upon what the supervisors and teacher already know about each other and their previous working relationship. Therefore, the interactional behavior will be different with each person. Whatever the relationship that exists, the supervisor must be careful not to do or say anything in the pre-observation conference that is likely to unsettle the teacher before the class begins.

The major intent of the pre-observation conference is for the supervisor to get a clear idea about what will take place in the lesson to be observed. It is an inappropriate time for the supervisor to make value judgments about the expected effectiveness of the upcoming lesson.

Before the pre-observation conference the supervisor and teacher should set a definite time for the classroom observation by the supervisor. Making an appointment with the teacher for the supervisory visit will tend to dispel the inspector image of supervision. The supervisor is conveying the position that he is not trying to catch the teacher at his worst but allowing the teacher to adequately prepare and perform at his best.

We realize that supervisors, administrators, and teachers are working on a very tight schedule. Because of the time consideration it is important for the pre-observation conference to be scheduled several days in advance of the actual meeting. We have found that the conference can be conducted in about ten minutes. This is a sufficient amount of time to cover all of the important points in the conference. Some school districts have developed forms which facilitate the pre-observation conference and help to conserve time. The forms can be most helpful but we are most emphatic in our belief that a completed form should not take the place of a face to face conference. See Figure 2 for an example of the pre-observation conference form used by several schools and districts.

Although building trust and being sensitive to the needs of the teacher are overriding concerns in the pre-observation conference, the supervisor must also be sensitive to his own needs and motivations. This attention can help prevent the supervisor from saying things that are satisfying to his own ego needs, but preventing real acceptance of what the teacher is communicating.

Too, building trust is usually accomplished by performance rather than mere verbalization. In other words, the behavior the supervisor exhibits over a series of classroom observations and conferences, rather than during one single visit, will determine the degree of trust that evolves between the supervisor and the teacher.

As the supervisor explains the specific steps that are involved in the supervisory process, emphasis should be placed on what will be taking place during the observation. For example, the supervisor should point out that he will be doing a lot of writing and recording of what is observed. Assurance should also be made that this written record will be the basis for the post-observation conference.

CONTENT OF THE CONFERENCE

The specific areas to be discussed in the pre-observation were presented in summary form earlier. It is not necessary to discuss each area in the order presented but it is important that all areas are discussed and understood by both the supervisor and the teacher. A detailed description of the pre-observation activities is presented in the balance of this chapter.

Class Setting

The initial phase of the conference can be an excellent time for the supervisor to become better acquainted with the teacher's perception of

PRE-OBSERVATION CONFERENCE

Teacher _____

Date _____

Grade/Subject _____

Observer _____

1. Class Setting

2. Objectives

3. Student Characteristics/Evaluation

4. Methods and Materials

5. Supervisory Role

Figure 2. Form used for pre-observation conference.

the curriculum. As the class setting is discussed the supervisor might ask such questions as:

a. What is the general area of study?
b. What program goals or objectives are reflected in this area of study?
c. Are these program goals related to the school or district goals?
d. How does the instruction to be observed fit in with the area of study?

The answers to these questions should help the supervisor get a general orientation about the upcoming observation. The questions should not be asked in an interrogatory sense but in a clarifying manner. The amount of clarification about the class setting needed will vary depending on how close the supervisor is to the instructional program.

Clarifying the Objectives

Most teachers have purposes for their classroom instruction. Early in the pre-observation conference the supervisor and the teacher should review both the process and content objectives that the teacher has for the lesson. By content objectives, we mean learner outcome objectives. Or to put it another way, what the student will be able to learn as a result of the lesson. Process objectives are those objectives that the teacher has specified about what the students will be doing while the learning is taking place. For example, the teacher may have a process objective whereby all students are expected to take an active part in a discussion.

Although the teacher probably has some general expectations for the class it is necessary to clarify the objectives in terms of learner outcomes. At this point the supervisor will need to be an "active listener" and will need to make use of the paraphrasing skill discussed earlier.

The objectives clarification process is depicted in the following discussion.

Supervisor: "What are your objectives for the lesson?"
Teacher: "I will be teaching the causes of the Civil War."
Supervisor: "Then you want the students to be able to identify the causes of the Civil War?"
Teacher: "Well, more than that. I want them to be able to identify and analyze the causes as to their relative importance."
Supervisor: "I understand your content objective and I would also like to know what the students will be doing while they are identifying and analyzing the causes of the Civil War."

Teacher: "I expect them to listen to my presentation during the first part of the class and then they will meet in small groups to discuss and analyze what was presented."

Supervisor: "As I understand it, all students are to listen to the lecture, then take part in the small group discussions."

Teacher: "That's right."

As this brief discussion took place, several points were clarified. The teacher began with what he was going to do. The clarification process shifted the focus from the teacher to the students. The content objective was re-stated in terms of learner expectations. Note that the objective was not stated totally in behavioral terms. However, it was clear that there were both low cognitive and high cognitive expectations. Finally, it was specified what the students would be doing (process objective) while they were attending to the content objective.

Learner Characteristics and Evaluation

After clarifying the objectives, the supervisor should ask if any prerequisite skills or understandings are needed by the students in order to accomplish the objectives. This step in the pre-observation conference is a check to make sure that thought has been given to a pre-assessment of where the students are relative to the expected outcomes.

We have found that this is often the teacher's weakest area in planning instruction. Not enough attention has been given to whether or not students have mastered prerequisites. This area of the conference provides an opportunity to discuss pre-assessment as an important planning activity.

It should be pointed out that pre-assessment does not have to be in the form of paper and pencil tests. There are a variety of ways to pre-assess depending on the type of class, characteristics of the learners, and the instructional objectives. For example, a teacher may determine readiness by observing students working on the previous material. A class discussion could also give the teacher information about readiness. Results from tests on previous material may also be helpful in the pre-assessment process.

Whatever strategy is used (or combination of strategies) it is essential for the teacher to know which students are ready to give attention to the learning objectives. Problems of motivation and apathy are often a result of having students attempt to learn new concepts without mastering prerequisite material.

The second important concern of this phase of the conference is to determine how the teacher plans to evaluate the achievement of the objectives. Once again, it is important to realize that there are a number of post-assessment procedures available to the teacher. Observation of the students during the lesson, an analysis of any student products from the lesson, and paper and pencil tests are examples of possible post-assessment activities.

It is very likely that the evaluation of student learning will take place some time after the observation. It is not necessary for the supervisor to formally observe the evaluation process. It is important that the supervisor knows how the evaluation activities are to be conducted and if the characteristics of the students have been taken into consideration.

Instructional Strategies and Materials

The pre-observation conference is a time when the teacher can briefly share with the supervisor those instructional strategies which probably will be used during the lesson. At this point, the supervisor should be careful not to make a value judgment about the appropriateness of the activities the teacher has selected. In some cases the teacher may volunteer information pertaining to the rationale for choosing a particular technique or approach. For example, certain unusual circumstances may exist in the classroom and the teacher may wish to explain these to the supervisor.

It is important to distinguish between teacher strategy and student expectations. The focus in this phase of the conference is on what the teacher will be doing and the materials needed to conduct the lesson. The possibilities are obviously quite numerous. The teacher may be planning on: a lecture; a lecture discussion; a demonstration; student directed learning with the teacher as a facilitator; or any number of instructional strategies.

The materials to be used may range from textbooks and chalkboards to learning centers. The instruction may be mediated through the use of overhead projectors, filmstrips, records, or whatever the teacher has available which will make the lesson more meaningful.

The classroom observation will be much more meaningful to the supervisor when he is aware of the instructional strategies and materials to be used. This information will also help in defining the role of the supervisor during the observation.

Supervisory Role

The final phase of the pre-observation conference is to reach agreement about the supervisory role or focus. It is impossible for one person to observe and record all that is going on in the classroom. We have found that the supervisor can focus either on student behavior or on teacher behavior. Sometimes it is not possible to record everything the students or teachers are doing. Therefore, we have delineated the observation process into teacher verbal or physical behavior and student verbal or physical behavior.

The behavior the supervisor focuses on should be based on the objectives of the lesson and the strategies and materials the teacher will use. If the teacher is going to conduct a discussion in order to attain certain cognitive objectives it would be logical for the supervisor to record teacher verbal behavior. It might even be possible to record teacher and student verbal depending on the pace of the lesson.

On the other hand if the teacher is acting as a facilitator to small groups it may be important for the supervisor to focus on student verbal and physical behavior. This focus could help in determining which students are taking part and those who are doing things that are not in keeping with the objectives.

We have found that a supervisor and teacher will conduct a good pre-observation conference up to this point. Then we find that not enough attention is given to the role of the supervisor during the observation. If the role is not clear and is not agreed upon, the observation will not be as helpful to the teacher as it can be. Further, the post-observation conference is highly dependent on the agreements reached during the pre-observation conference. So, it cannot be emphasized too strongly that the focus of the supervisor must be clear and that this focus is directly related to the objectives, strategies, and materials to be used during the observation.

Occasionally a supervisor will have agreed upon a specific role or focus and then find after the lesson has started that it would be more productive to focus on a different set of behaviors. This may be necessary for any number of reasons. Any change should have a sound rationale and should bear a relationship to the stated objectives. If the teacher and supervisor are working from a sound trust relationship a change in focus will not be seen as breaking an agreement but as an attempt to provide the teacher the most helpful kind of observation data.

Teachers being observed for the first time using the procedures described in this book find it difficult to suggest the best observation role for the supervisor. The supervisor will need to be able to suggest which role or roles might be most appropriate based on the information gathered during the pre-observation conference. After several visits we have found that teachers have very clear expectations about the supervisory role which are consistent with the lesson objectives and activities.

The write-up of the pre-observation conference does not need to be lengthy or hard to understand. Each phase of the conference should be summarized by the supervisor and teacher. If the school uses a form, the teacher may have used the form for lesson planning previous to the actual conference. However, the final summary should be written by the supervisor from the information provided by the teacher. This will help to give assurance that the supervisor has a clear understanding about what will take place in the lesson to be observed.

Figures 3, 4, and 5 are examples of actual pre-observation conference write-ups. These summaries were based on information given to the supervisors during the pre-observation conferences. A review of these examples may help to give the reader some ideas about the length and specificity needed for a write-up. In the following chapters the classroom observations and post-observation conferences related to these write-ups have been presented and discussed.

SUMMARY

The pre-observation conference is a critical step in the supervisory program. We take the position that every classroom observation aimed at improving instruction should be preceded by a well organized pre-observation conference. This conference does not need to take a lot of time. It has been shown over and over again that all of the conference areas suggested in this chapter can be discussed in about ten minutes. This may be the most valuable time spent in the entire supervisory process.

The supervisory program should be aimed at improving instruction. When the teacher and supervisor: discuss the class setting; clarify objectives; describe student characteristics and the evaluation process; discuss instructional strategies and materials; and agree on the supervisory role there are numerous opportunities to improve instructional planning on a cooperative basis.

The cooperative process described in this chapter offers one vehicle for actualizing positive working relationships. Healthy, productive organizations are dependent on this type of interaction. Certainly, schools are no exception. Instructional programs will more likely be improved in schools where working relationships are positive and the process is synergetic.

DEVELOPMENT AND RENEWAL ACTIVITIES

1. Read *Stating Behavioral Objectives for Classroom Instruction* by Norman Gronlund to get a clear understanding about using objectives in teaching. This is an inexpensive paperback published by the Macmillan Co. in 1970.

PRE-OBSERVATION CONFERENCE

Teacher ___Mrs. W.___

Date ___1/30/75___

Grade/Subject ___6th—Language Arts___

Observer ___E. C. B.___

1. **Class Setting**

    6th grade Language/Arts Mental Health Class. A combination of two content areas to integrate content and process.

2. **Objectives**

    Clarify and improve self-concept. Utilize good discussion skills (avoid over-participation). Involve most class members.

3. **Student Characterstics/Evaluation**

    Full ability range. One group reading below grade level, one reading above. One hyperactive child. Students have discussed skills necessary for clear communication. Have held other discussion sessions and evaluated these. Over-participation has been discussed with some individuals. Evaluation will be informal. The group will assess their ability to discuss. Individuals will evaluate their own progress as group members.

4. **Methods and Materials**

    Students will share objects important to their family and explain flags they have designed to represent their background.

    Students will discuss the influence of family on self concept and their behavior at school and as a class.

5. **Supervisory Role**

    Focus on student responses to teacher verbal. Also identify those who volunteer information.

Figure 3. Pre-observation conference for 6th Grade language arts/mental health class.

PRE-OBSERVATION CONFERENCE

Teacher ___Mrs. P.___

Date ___10/20/75___

Grade/Subject ___Senior Elective—Political Systems___

Observer ___J.B.___

1. Class Setting

Senior elective course (some juniors) on Comparative Political Systems. Have been comparing governments based on five concepts. Currently on political decision-makers. Materials and activities in Friday class set the stage for today.

2. Objective

Have small groups (based on previous activities) make a decision, a judgment, and know why—associating interest groups with fictitious political candidates.

3. Student Characteristics/Evaluation

Students have been involved in developing their positions. Informal evaluation based on today's discussion. Some assessment in unit exam.

4. Methods and Materials

Use Fenton's inquiry materials—process oriented teacher will serve as "manager of the class." Use chalkboard, handout materials and book.

5. Supervisory Role

Chart interaction of students and teacher during discussion.

Figure 4. Pre-observation conference for class on comparative political systems.

PRE-OBSERVATION CONFERENCE

Teacher ___Ms. C.___

Date ___10/17/73___

Grade/Subject ___11th—English Literature___

Observer ___J. B.___

1. Class Setting

High School English Literature Class. Unit on poetry.

2. Objectives

Students will be able to identify important ideas (from poem) and relate them to their own lives. Expected that all students will take part in the discussion.

3. Student Characteristics/Evaluation

Students have had introduction to material earlier in the unit. All but one or two are ready for this material. Evaluation will take place at the end of the period and selected items will be included in the final exam.

4. Methods and Materials

Record of the poem "To a Mouse" will be played. Teacher will conduct a discussion about the poem.

5. Supervisory Role

Supervisor will focus on the verbal behavior of the teacher.

Figure 5. Pre-observation conference for English literature class.

It also includes a summary of the taxonomies in the affective, cognitive, and psychomotor domains.

2. Generate a number of instructional objectives and share them with a colleague. Discuss the appropriateness of these objectives for a given area of instruction.

3. Practice paraphrasing (active listening) with several colleagues. Clarify what the other person is trying to communicate to you before you give any feedback. Content for a paraphrasing session might be helping one another delineate instructional goals and objectives for a specific lesson.

4. Many school districts intermediate units, and colleges have the Instructional Program filmstrips developed by James W. Popham and produced by Vimcet Associates, Inc., P.O. Box 24714, Los Angeles, California. If these are available select those that relate to objectives, instructional decising-making, and evaluation, for review and analysis.

5. Follow the steps for the pre-observation conference discussed in this chapter and role play a conference with a colleague. Record the conference on a tape recorder to use for a careful analysis of your conferencing behavior.

Chapter 5

The Classroom Observation

This chapter is based on the assumption that people in school organizations are assigned to supervisory responsibilities without adequate—or perhaps any—preparation in the skills of classroom observation. Activities and processes are described that can help improve the skills necessary for meaningful classroom observation. The emphasis is upon techniques to assist in observing a lesson, so that an evaluation of that which was observed can be used in a more objective, systematic, helpful, and effective manner to improve instruction.

OBSERVATION LIMITATIONS

While the idea of observing a lesson seems somewhat transparent at the outset, several problems in perception have been identified which can significantly affect any observer, and, therefore, his observations. Examples of these problems are perception isolation and perceptual bias. In essence, these phenomena can reduce the perceptual effectiveness of the observer.

Perception isolation is a limitation on sensory intake resulting from increased threat. The individual reacts to a multitude of stimuli in a threatening situation by eliminating many of the stimuli and focusing on those which will protect him in the situation. Thus, the observer may react to the threatening situation by looking only for the positive elements of the lesson. These could then be indicated to the instructor and a potentially difficult session avoided. A more negatively oriented individual may observe only the actions he doesn't like and use them to attack the teacher. These two approaches are equally ineffective, if one's purpose is to help the teacher and facilitate instructional improvement.

Perceptional bias is the distortion of perception resulting from the influence of the observer's personal attitudes and past experiences. This process has been referred to as perceptual readiness. Here, pre-experiences tend to limit and interpret that which is seen so that it fits a particular way of observing the world. A typical example, (and one used in many research studies), is to provide a film of two people, (black and white, tall and short, man and woman), talking in an agitated manner. Perceptual bias will tend to interpret that discussion and place blame or intent on one or the other of the individuals involved. Therefore, it might be said that our prejudices tend to color our views of the world in general and our impressions of a classroom lesson in particular. What we see, perhaps, is what we are prepared to see.

In order to neutralize the effects of both perceptual isolation and perceptual bias, the classroom observer is advised to focus on the production of an objective record of behavior while in the classroom. It was pointed out in the discussion of the pre-observation conference that the behaviors observed in the classroom may be those of the teacher or of the learners, and they may be either verbal behaviors or physical behaviors. The purpose of the observation is to reduce to a written or diagrammed record a specified and determined set of observable behaviors occurring during the teacher-learning act. The analysis and evaluation of this record is to be delayed until the post-observation conference. The task for the observer in the classroom is to record actual observable events or behaviors.

OBSERVATION TECHNIQUES

A traditional recommendation to novice supervisors has been never to write while you are in the classroom. If the teacher sees the observer solely as an evaluator, this may be an appropriate warning. Some teachers will begin to place undue weight on any note taking. As a result, when the observer suddenly looks down and writes furiously during a lesson, these teachers can become concerned about the behavior that might have produced such an interest on the part of the observer. The teacher may then find himself watching for and over-reacting to these bursts of supervisory interest and a less effective lesson may result.

In the supervision process that we propose, events are recorded as continuously as possible. The result can be the same as not writing at all. The teacher will not be directed toward particular activities of the supervisor because no special behaviors, either good or bad, are isolated for the record. Too, the supervisor has told the teacher during the pre-observation conference that he would be writing continuously and what this writing would entail. Most important, the teacher knows this written record will be shared with him.

The supervisor should locate himself in the room where he can observe most of the students and the teacher and then write or diagram for a given period of time. Experience has shown that the development of these recording skills can be learned and improved through regular practice. A supervisor just starting this system may find it difficult to record for more than fifteen to twenty minutes at a time. As supervisors increase the number of observations they do, the easier they will find it to record what is going on in an accurate and non-judgmental manner.

The major purpose of the classroom observation is to produce a record of the behaviors which occur in the classroom. These behaviors must be recorded in neutral or objective terms. They should be recorded without assumed intentions or value judgments. For example, if a student reaches out and pats the shoulder of another student, the observer should note that the shoulder was tapped or touched. The observer should not record that the student was bothered, harrassed, intimidated, or use other terms which imply a non-observable intent.

Earlier, it was suggested that the supervisor will be able to focus on the verbal or physical behavior of the teacher and students. It may even be necessary to focus on just one type of behavior for either the teacher or the students. In either case, it is essential that the observation record be non-judgmental and as accurate as possible.

Observing and Recording

In the pre-observation conference, agreement is reached about the supervisory role or focus. This agreement has set the stage for the supervisor going into the classroom. If the focus is to be on a discussion, then the supervisor should be prepared to record verbal behavior. If the focus is to be on some of the physical activity, then the supervisor should be prepared to chart or diagram what the students are doing or what the teacher is doing. With practice, a supervisor will be able to record or chart nearly all of the physical behavior in the classroom.

Supervisors often ask about charting and recording systems. We have found that it is best for each person to work out his own system. This system should be easy to use and easy to interpret in the post-observation conference. In the balance of this chapter we have presented sample verbal and physical records we have made during classroom observations. We would suggest that these records be carefully reviewed in terms of the recording process. This review should give potential observers sufficient direction to begin the recording process.

Figure 6 is an observation record or chart which depicts student responses to teacher directed questions. The pre-observation conference write-up for this lesson was shown in Figure 3, Chapter 4.

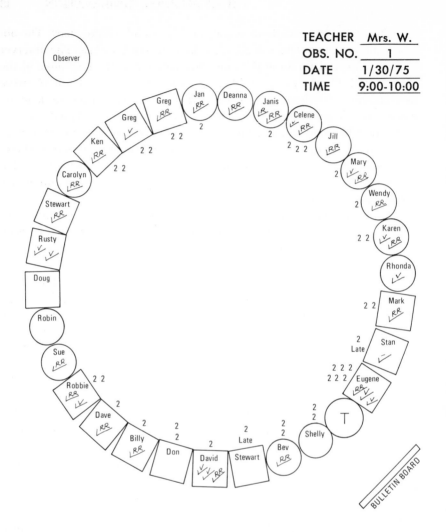

TEACHER Mrs. W.
OBS. NO. ____1____
DATE   1/30/75
TIME   9:00-10:00

CODE:

RR — responds to request

V — volunteers

— refused request

2 — participated in discussion/2nd strategy

Figure 6. Record of student responses in large group discussion.

The observer's code is shown at the bottom left of the chart. The observer did not have a seating chart before entering the class. The observer quickly made a diagram of the room arrangement at the beginning of the class period. Circles denoted where girls were seated and squares were used for boys. As the class proceeded the teacher called the students by name. The observer wrote the names in as the lesson developed.

From the chart, the teacher and observer will be able to determine: which students responded to requests; who refused to respond to direct questions; and which students volunteered information. This information is consistent with the agreement made in the pre-observation conference about the observer's role for this lesson.

Figure 7 is an observation record which focused on the interaction of students, groups of students, and the teacher in an inquiry oriented lesson. The pre-observation conference for this lesson was shown in Figure 4, Chapter 4.

Once again the classroom diagram was quickly sketched at the beginning of the class. Squares were used for boys and circles for girls. Not all of the students were called by name so only those clearly heard by the supervisor were recorded. The code is self-explanatory. The movement of the teacher was also recorded. This is shown by the arrows around the teacher. Marks across the arrows indicate more time was spent in that location than in the others. The letters CR represent choral responses by the class.

The information from this chart will help the supervisor and teacher determine: which students responsed to teacher initiated questions; which students initiated questions to the teacher; the amount of response from individual students; the amount of response from the groups; and the position of the teacher in relation to the groups. The information generated from this chart is supportive of the supervisory role established in the pre-observation conference.

When the supervisor has agreed to focus on verbal behavior the procedure for gathering the data is rather clear. The supervisor must attempt to write down everything that is said by either the students or the teacher. This is a skill which requires regular practice and the use of techniques to shorten or abbreviate words. Another technique is to omit part of the discussion when the supervisor starts getting behind with the writing. This can be shown in the notes by using several dots (e.g. . . .) to indicate gaps in the dialogue. It is expected that during the post-observation conference the teacher and supervisor can reconstruct the discussion and fill in most of the missing information.

In Chapter 4, Figure 5, a pre-observation conference write-up was

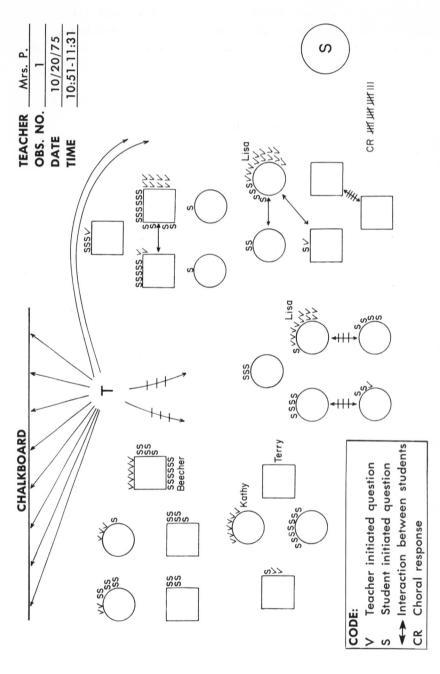

Figure 7. Student teacher interaction during inquiry lesson.

TEACHER __Mrs. P.__
OBS. NO. __1__
DATE __10/20/75__
TIME __10:51-11:31__

CHALKBOARD

Beecher

Kathy

Terry

Lisa

Lisa

CR ⅢⅡ ⅢⅡ ⅢⅡ III

CODE:
V   Teacher initiated question
S   Student initiated question
↔ Interaction between students
CR Choral response

presented for a class in English Literature. It was agreed that the supervisor would focus on the verbal behavior of the teacher during the observation. The verbal record of that observation is presented below. The teacher's dialogue is written out. Student response is indicated by the letter SR. When there was a group response the letters CR were used.

Teacher	Students
You remember what we did the first day of class? We mentioned Robert Burns.	CR
Look at the poem, "To a Mouse," page 233 in your books. Anyone tell me what the poem is about?	SR
The first day of class we talked about "To a Louse."	
In the poem, "'To a Mouse," a small creature is used to teach a lesson . . . . a moral lesson.	
I want you to listen to a record (To a Mouse). Then we will go over each stanza. And I will explain the lesson. (Record)	
Let's take the first stanza. He was reading in a Scottish dialect. I'll read it even though I don't have a dialect . . . . What do you know, Beth?	SR
Raise your hand please. (Poem read) What one word would let you know the meaning? Chip?	SR
Murdering? Go back before that.	
What does the word, loathe, mean? It would not be a compliment. (Poem read)	CR
Do you know at this point why Burns is talking about the mouse being Mortal? Andy?	SR
Okay. Someone else.	SR
What is he saying that this mouse is doing? (Poem read)	CR

What is this stanza saying, Vicki?   SR

(Poem read)

Explain the stanza, Sharon.   SR

Okay, say it again and speak up this time. Okay, thank
you.   SR

(Poem read)

What's he trying to make you realize at this point?
Mike?

You scratching your head or raising your hand?   SR

Wasn't a house just constructed and it took a long time
to make it?

(Poem read)

Okay, so just as a mouse thought he would have a safe
house, man has visions destroyed. Beth, very good.   SR

(Poem read)

Ronnie, what's the difference between the mouse and
man?   SR

All right. What are the lines in the poem you are familiar with?   CR

Raise your hands.

Three people? Forget about the lines, what thought is
important?

The rest of you have no idea, Chuck?   SR

Okay, let me put in another way. What is universal?
In terms of the main thoughts?

How many of you think you could point out the important lines?

The rest have no idea?

Okay, Ellen, what are the lines?   SR

Those of you without your hand up, have you never
heard of them?

Okay, then, I taught you something today!

Can you give me some examples from your own experiences?   SR

Have to do anything with *Mice and Men?* It's been so long since I've read the book I can't answer that. Have you read the book lately?	SR
Okay, Vicki.	
Can't you put it on your level—personal. Something or an incident that made your plans go astray?	
You don't like to recite personal instances in class?	CR
No one can think of an example?	
Okay.	SR
Okay, good, Barry. You study, study and fail the test. The best laid plans go astray. So your plans did go astray.	SR
I was planning on being out of my apartment in my house six weeks ago. My best laid plans went astray. Every day something we plan goes astray.	
Andy?	SR
A bit lengthy? You thing the best laid plans is enough?	SR
Which lines should be left out? Point out the specific lines.	CR

Lesson began 2:45, this activity lasted until 3:02.

Board Work and Student Discussion until 3:08.

The objectives of the English Literature lesson specified the importance of how well the students would be able to process the discussion information. Because the teacher verbal behavior would have a strong influence on the student outcomes it was agreed that the supervisor should focus on what the teacher was saying. As a result of the verbal record the teacher and supervisor should be able to determine: which students were called on; the type of questions used by the teacher; the amount of verbal reinforcement; and any verbal idiosyncratic patterns used by the teacher.

SUMMARY

There are limitations to how much information can be gathered during a classroom observation. The amount of information recorded will largely depend on the skill of the supervisor. As a supervisor conducts more observations the data gathering skills will be improved. However, the perception problems will need to be recognized and taken into account by teachers and supervisors.

When the pre-observation conference is done well, the supervisor will be better prepared to do a good observation. Having a clear understanding about what is going to happen in class will facilitate the observation activities. Most important, the supervisor has a specified role to play. Accurate, non-judgmental, observing and recording is easier to achieve when the focus is clear.

There are a number of recording processes used in various observation systems. In order to get the kind of data described in this chapter the supervisor should develop his own coding and charting system. When verbal behavior is recorded it is necessary to write down as much as possible using procedures which will make lesson reconstruction as accurate as possible.

Finally, there is only one way to become a skilled observer and that is to observe and record as many lessons as possible. It is surprising how quickly a supervisor develops the skills necessary to record a significant amount of accurate, helpful, instructional data.

DEVELOPMENT AND RENEWAL ACTIVITIES

1. Practice recording short (five minutes to ten minutes) observations focusing on the verbal or physical behavior of teachers and students.
2. Have a colleague record the same segment of a lesson that you record. Compare the information you get and if your records are different try to determine the reasons.
3. When in a committee meeting or listening to speeches, try to improve your observation and recording skills.

Chapter 6

The Post-Observation Conference

The practice of having a conference to discuss a classroom observation or visitation is still not generally accepted by supervisors and administrators. There are still many instances where the teacher is observed by a supervisor and then is not given an opportunity to have any feedback about the observation. Sometimes there is delayed feedback which is given during an annual or semi-annual personnel conference. When this occurs there is very little chance that the transaction will help to improve instruction.

The post-observation conference should provide the opportunity to build good working relationships. The intent of the conference is to utilize the thinking of at least two persons concerned about instruction to bring about desired changes.

The teacher and the supervisor bring their perceptions about the instruction to the conference. Each person has an opportunity to check and clarify his perceptions about: what has happened; what needs to be improved; practice that needs to be continued; and resources that may be helpful in bring about desired changes.

In a general sense, the supervisor and teacher are able to conduct an instructional needs assessment during the post-observation conference. They review what was expected to take place and what actually happened. The gap between what was hoped for and the actual results constitutes an instructional need. When needs are identified efforts can be concentrated on meeting or fulfilling the needs. In this entire process the instructional analysis skills of the conference participants will be renewed.

There is an ideal place and time for the post-observation conference. If at all possible the conference should be held in the classroom after the students have left. There are a number of advantages in meeting in the room. The most important one is that it is very helpful during the lesson reconstruction phase. In addition, this removes the problems associated with meeting in an administrative office where superior-subordinate attitudes are reinforced.

The ideal time for the post-observation conference is immediately after the observation. This will significantly increase the probability of reaching agreement about what took place. It will also be much easier to fill in any gaps in the observation record.

Sufficient time should be set aside for the conference. The amount of time needed will vary and depends on a number of factors. In order not to rush through the conference and perhaps miss some key points, at least forty-five minutes should be scheduled for this activity.

By having a specific format for the post-observation conference, a number of safeguards are built into the process. There is a more efficient and effective use of the time spent. Cooperative processes are inherent in the conference. The analysis will be more comprehensive and there will be a number of alternative solutions for any problems which are identified. For these and other reasons, the specific steps in the post-observation conference and the recommended sequence for the conference have been presented in the balance of this chapter.

LESSON RECONSTRUCTION

The first phase of the post-observation conference should be devoted to reconstructing what took place during the observation. The supervisor should begin by sharing what was recorded during the lesson. It is often a good idea to first restate the supervisory role which was agreed upon during the pre-observation conference. This is especially helpful if the pre-observation conference took place the day preceding the observation.

If the observation focus was on the verbal behavior of either the teacher or the students the observation record will consist of a running account of what was said. It was pointed out earlier that it is highly unlikely that the record will be complete. By carefully reviewing what was recorded the teacher can help the observer fill in any gaps in the record. There may also be some statements which were not clear to the observer so this was an opportunity to clarify what was said. However, value judgments about the record should not be made during the reconstruction process.

When the supervisory focus is on the physical behavior in the classroom the observation record will probably be similar to the charts or diagrams presented in chapter six. Reconstructing the physical behavior is usually much easier and takes less time. In most cases, it is also easier to be accurate when charting physical behavior. Once again the record should be shared with the teacher so that the teacher will have an opportunity to give additional information. This will help to assure that the record is as complete as possible and at the same time demonstrate that this is a cooperative process.

When the record of the lesson has been reconstructed to the satisfaction of the conference participants the stage has been set for the remainder of the conference. It is always a good idea to verbalize this agreement before going on. There have been instances where agreement was assumed and it turned out to be a false assumption. If this happens there is little chance that the conference will be productive.

PATTERN IDENTIFICATION

A pattern is defined as any behavior or action which seems to recur. After the lesson has been reconstructed the teacher and supervisor should analyze the record in order to identify physical or verbal patterns. The patterns should emerge from the record and should not be pre-determined.

Many patterns have emerged from the analyses of observation records. Those which seem to occur most often are summarized in Figure 8. Note that the patterns are clustered according to the type of behavior and in relation to the teacher and the students.

The question asking pattern will be apparent in any verbal record of a teacher directed discussion. The teacher may ask questions which call for specific bits of information. When this is done regularly a pattern of questioning will emerge. This is often referred to as a convergent questioning pattern.

Another type of questioning pattern which may emerge from the data is often referred to as a divergent pattern. This pattern is the result of questions which cause students to analyze, synthesize ,or evaluate information. It is quite possible that a teacher will exhibit both types of questioning patterns during a discussion. From the verbal record it is also possible to identify the sequence of questions. This would constitute an additional verbal pattern.

Verbal reinforcement patterns are also easily identified in an analysis of the verbal record. A variety of words which give verbal reinforcement may be used by the teacher. Clustered together they represent a pattern. For example, words and phrases such as: good answer; excellent; very good; that's right on; all give verbal reinforcement. A negative pattern may also emerge which consists of words and phrases that do not reinforce but which may be considered aversive.

Anyone that engages in a considerable amount of dialogue will probably develop verbal idiosyncratic patterns. Words or phrases that appear regularly but do not seem to be related to the content of the discussion

Teacher Behavior	Student Behavior
Verbal Behavior	Verbal Behavior
1. Control of groups and individuals 2. Question asking 3. Response to students 4. Reinforcement procedures 5. Amount of talk; sequence of oral participation 6. Verbal idiosyncracies	1. Sequence of response 2. Location of response in room 3. Amount and level of questions 4. Initiation procedures 5. Inter-student comments
Physical Behavior	Physical Behavior

1. Placement in room
   —re: student responses
   —re: student participation
2. Gestures
3. Use of AV equipment
4. Use of chalkboard
	1. Hand raising
	
	2. Movement around room
	3. Movement in seats
	4. Grouping

Figure 8.   Frequently observed behavior patterns.

may be viewed as idiosyncratic. The possibilities are too numerous to list but they become obvious when a verbal record is analyzed.

Student verbal patterns which occur rather frequently include the sequence of responses to a teacher and the student to student comments. It is not uncommon to find that a small group of students are controlling a discussion. They may volunteer information without being called on or it may be the result of a combination of factors. Teachers get into a pattern of directing their discussion at a few students in the classroom and these students are the ones that usually have the information that the teacher wants.

Student to student comments emerge as patterns in a number of ways. Two or three students may exchange verbal information throughout a lesson which may or may not have to do with the content of the lesson. Informal student leadership patterns emerge throughout the course of a school year. Gradually these students may control a great deal of the classroom activity with their comments to other students.

The most common physical pattern of the teacher has to do with position and movement in the room. Sometimes a teacher will establish a movement pattern which keeps certain students out of contact over a long period of time. This same pattern may be such that small clusters of students are in regular contact with the teacher. This often occurs during laboratory and activity classes.

The use of the chalkboard will often have an influence on the movement pattern of the teacher. A teacher may have established a routine of lecturing and writing on the board or getting information from the students and recording it on the board. The sequence of movement and use of the board may emerge as a physical pattern.

A physical pattern may not always have to do with movement. Instead there may be a position or place in the room that is regularly occupied by the teacher. Sitting behind the desk, on the desk, or standing behind a lectern, are examples of a position pattern.

Student physical patterns which are quite common include their movement around the room and the way they are grouped or positioned in the classroom. Student movement patterns occur more frequently in the lower grades as well as in activity and laboratory classes. Whether the students select their own seats or they are assigned to seats or groups, the way they are organized in the classroom often emerges as a physical pattern.

A few selected examples have been presented in order to clarify what is meant by teacher and student verbal and physical patterns. Many different patterns are identified through the use of the observation record. The patterns will vary depending on the unique characteristics of the teacher, students, and school setting.

Patterns standing alone have little value. It is easy to fall into the trap of making value judgments about the appropriateness of certain patterns when they are first identified in the record. It is essential that patterns be cooperatively assessed in terms of their relative importance.

PATTERN ASSESSMENT

After the patterns have been identified it is possible to determine their influence on the instructional process. The first step in pattern assessment is to restate and review the objectives for the lesson. Both content and process objectives will be influenced by the patterns.

Pattern assessment is highly judgmental. Inferences will be drawn and relationships identified and analyzed. The teacher may have had a process objective for involving all of the students in a class or group in a class discussion. The patterns may indicate that this was not accomplished.

It may have been due to the position of the teacher, movement in the room, or the way the questions were asked. The supervisor and teacher will need to assess all of the information they have to determine which patterns interfered with achievement of the objective.

A content objective for a class may have been stated which identified what the students would learn during the lesson. Verbal patterns may indicate that some of the students did master the material while others did not demonstrate what they had learned. The way the information was presented may have had an adverse effect on some students. The verbal lecture and discussion patterns may actually have interfered with the student learning. Once again it will be the responsibility of the teacher and supervisor to determine how the patterns supported or interfered with the intended learning.

It is easy for the teacher and supervisor to develop the pattern of discussing only those behaviors which interfered with or did not help in meeting the objectives. It is very important to identify and discuss those patterns which helped the students achieve the objectives. These helpful patterns need to be reinforced so that they will continue to be used when the objectives are appropriate.

A summary of the patterns identified in a lesson should be made. This record will be useful to the teacher and supervisor as they plan instructional changes based on the pattern assessment. A form that has been helpful for developing a summary of the patterns and other observation information is presented in Figure 9.

PLANNING FUTURE INSTRUCTION

Simply identifying patterns of behavior and analyzing them in terms of the teacher's objectives has little value. Improvement of instruction comes only with changes in behavior, and changes in behavior should be planned.

The patterns either enhance, impede, or have no effect on the attainment of the objectives. Once the patterns have been identified and analyzed the supervisor and the teacher are ready to plan for future instruction. This planning process may also become the next pre-observation conference.

As the supervisor and the teacher plan for future instruction, they may agree about alternative behaviors that will strengthen the instruction. They must be careful not to focus only on changing behavior that impeded the attainment of objectives. The concept of change also includes strengthening appropriate behaviors, and the planning for future instruction should

Learning Objectives _____

— Patterns —

Teacher

Student

Verbal

Physical

TEACHER _____
DATE _____
TIME _____ TO _____
OBSERVATION NO. _____

Recommendations:

Signatures:

_____
Teacher

_____
Observer

Figure 9. Pattern summary sheet.

55

include positive discussion about the enhancing behaviors of the teacher.

Planning for future instruction can be a relatively simple step or it may become quite complex, depending upon what the analysis of instruction has revealed. For example, if most of the teacher's behavior has been enhancing with the exception of a verbal idiosyncratic pattern then simply identifying this pattern may cause the teacher to change. However, if the teacher is concerned with the lack of student-teacher interaction, the future instruction may include the use of various instructional strategies discussed and agreed upon during the post-observation conference.

A teacher who has trouble introducing the lesson may plan to use the micro-teaching technique. Thus, the planning for future instruction is really the process of developing a plan for changing behavior patterns. This may involve any number of possible activities, ranging from pointing out a particular pattern to the teacher to a series of in-depth sessions in various instructional methods.

One important side effect of this final phase of the post-observation conference is the opportunity to discuss staff development needed by the teacher and others on the instructional staff. The patterns identified during a series of observations of the faculty may indicate that there are some common instructional development needs. It may be found that there is an interest and need for several teachers to improve their discussion techniques. There may be general interest and need for information and techniques about grouping in the classroom. Staff development will be more meaningful when it results from the instructional needs of the teachers.

Staff development is also very important for supervisors. Administrators and supervisors have found that when they are expected to make recommendations during the post-observation conference they do not have an adequate information base. Rather than attempt to cover up when this occurs the supervisor should indicate that he will attempt to get the information needed to help the teacher improve.

The summary of the post-observation conference should include recommendations agreed upon by the teacher and the supervisor. Patterns which should be continued should be noted. Those which need to be improved or changed should also be noted. The resources needed for improvement should also be identified.

Finally, one full observation cycle may be helpful to a teacher. However, regular observations which are planned and based on the initial experience will help to bring about long term instructional improvement.

SUMMARY

A conference with the teacher following a classroom observation should be expected if not required. It is unfortunate that some school districts have had to mandate the conferences. The teacher and supervisor should see the post-observation conference as an opportunity to discuss, analyze, and develop plans for instructional improvement. It should not be seen as carrying out a policy which is time-consuming and bothersome.

More time needs to be scheduled for supervisors and teachers to share their instructional concerns. The post-observation conference provides an excellent opportunity to engage in a discussion about improvement needed in the entire educational program. The relationship of the school curriculum to the instructional process can provide the incentive for a comprehensive examination of all influences on the students. This examination can begin as a result of the conference discussion.

Identifying and assessing instructional needs is a two way process. That is, teachers and supervisors will find that they have similar gaps in their instructional knowledge. The cooperative processes related to the observation program can be extended to planning and taking part in staff development activities.

Summaries of post-observation conferences are an important source of data for the evaluation program. Important areas or categories for evaluation may result from information derived during the post-observation activities. Patterns which are frequently identified as being important in meeting certain objectives may be the focus of the classroom evaluation instrument. The relationship of the observation program to the evaluation program is described in chapter seven.

DEVELOPMENT AND RENEWAL ACTIVITIES

1. Review and analyze the observation records presented in chapter five to identify the important teacher and student patterns.
2. Identify tools which may be helpful in specific observation activities. For example, review category systems such as Interaction Analysis to determine how they may be helpful in the observation process.
3. View a video tape or a filmed lesson. Identify the patterns that can be observed. Role play a post-observation conference based on the information you have gathered.
4. Teach a short lesson to a colleague. Help conduct a post-observation conference of your teaching. Plan a future lesson from this experience.

Chapter 7

The Evaluation Program

The evaluation program of any school district includes a heavy emphasis on the teacher's classroom activities. Unfortunately, there are many instances where the evaluation program is not congruent with the supervision process. It is extremely important that the classroom or teaching evaluation component of the total evaluation program be in complete harmony with the classroom supervision process.

This section is devoted to a discussion of the basic assumptions and guidelines necessary to develop a teacher evaluation system which is in line with the synergetic supervision program described in the preceding chapters. A sample evaluation instrument is presented which has been developed by one school district using the synergetic process. It is crucial for each school district to develop an evaluation instrument which emanates from its supervisory program and which is consistent with the total district program of evaluation.

ASSUMPTIONS ABOUT THE EVALUATION PROGRAM

The Teacher

There are several basic assumptions that have to do with the teacher and the evaluation of teaching. These assumptions set the stage for the evaluation program described throughout this section.

First, every teacher wants to be competent. Every teacher, therefore, has the desire to improve in the teaching act. There is strong evidenc to support the notion that the teacher's most important goal is to be seen as a competent professional. This assumption is consistent with research being done in business and industry about the importance of employees developing job satisfaction. Crucial to the development of this satisfaction is the feeling that employees are seen to be competent by those with whom they associate. Classroom teachers can derive a higher level of job satisfaction through activities which help them improve their teaching.

The second basic assumption about teachers is that the role of the teacher is complex and multi-dimensional. Teachers are expected to fulfill a variety of roles both in and out of the classroom. Those activities which take place in the classroom are complex and highly demanding. In addition to the classroom expectations teachers have many other roles to fulfill in the school organization. These roles include playground supervisor, hall monitor and a variety of other non-teaching responsibilities.

The third assumption about teachers is that the teaching act is a primary element in the overall role of the teacher. The word primary should be emphasized in that, in some school organizations, the teaching act becomes less important as other demands are placed on the teachers. Instructional improvement cannot take place unless the teaching act is seen as the highest priority in the overall role of the teacher.

Finally, accountability and improvement of instruction go hand in hand. It is not enough to demand that people be held accountable. Accountability has been defined as the ability to deliver on one's promises. If the promise of the school is to give excellent instruction then every means must be made available to facilitate the teachers in improving their own instruction.

The Supervisor

There are assumptions about the supervisor which must have common agreement in a school organization if the supervisor is to play a productive role in the instructional improvement program. It must be agreed that instructional evaluation is a continuous and ongoing supervisory responsibility. Evaluation cannot be seen as an occasional activity which takes place as a result of administrative policy. The supervisor must be seen as a person who has a continuous commitment to improving the instructional program. This commitment manifests itself in many ways. Heavy involvement in the day-to-day instructional program must be the highest priority for the supervisor.

The second assumption about the supervisor is that this person has the skills, attitudes and knowledge to function effectively in a leadership role. It is unfortunate when many supervisors have been given the title and the responsibility but do not have the skills necessary to function effectively in their positions. Therefore, it is incumbent upon the supervisor to maintain a program of personal self-renewal which is aimed at developing and maintaining the necessary skills and understandings to be an effective instructional leader. Without this type of commitment the supervisor soon becomes irrelevant.

The final assumption about the supervisor is that instructional improvement must be the primary goal of the supervisor. Those who work in schools know that many demands are made on each supervisor and administrator which have nothing to do with instructional improvement. These demands must be met in order for the organization to be maintained. However, the supervisor must give instructional improvement the highest priority in terms of time and effort in order to provide the best learning environment for each student in the school.

The Process

There are several assumptions about the evaluation process which must be agreed upon by all those involved in the evaluation program. First, instructional evaluation must encourage diversity in teaching behavior. It has been found that teachers who are most similar in the way they teach are often the poorest teachers. On the other hand, it has been shown that teachers who are most dissimilar are often the most effective. Therefore, supervisors, administrators, department heads, and master teachers must not encourage other teachers to teach the way they do. They should, as a matter of fact, encourage diversity and creativity in the teaching act.

The second assumption about the evaluation process is that multiple observations of teaching tend toward a greater reliability of actual teaching behavior. This contradicts the point made by those who say that an occasional visit to a classroom gives them a true picture of what is going on in the classroom. The more visitations made to a classroom the greater the possibility that what is seen is representative of the ongoing teaching behavior. It is not as important to spend long periods of time visiting occasionally in the classroom. Greater reliability is achieved if more visits are made for shorter periods of time.

The next assumption about the evaluation process is that techniques by which the effectiveness of teaching behavior is assessed must be adapted to the characteristics, needs, and organizational structure of an individual school or school district. It is obvious that the student population of each school is unique to that school. It is also obvious that the teachers in a given school are very different from teachers in other schools. Also, the organizational structure, formal or informal, varies from school to school. There may be similar kinds of organizational charts but the school will operate differently depending upon the type of administrators and the facilities and resources available to the school. Therefore, the evaluation program must take into consideration the differences that exist in each school.

The final assumption about the evaluation process is that classroom behavior patterns which are identified by teachers and administrators as being necessary for instructional improvement should form the basis for the evaluation of teaching. Less attention should be given to those factors about the teacher which have nothing to do with improved programs of instruction. Very often evaluation forms and charts used in various districts throughout the country concentrate on these external aspects and give little attention to the important classroom behaviors which constitute excellence in teaching.

The Evaluation Instrument

There are several important assumptions related to the instrument used in the evaluation process. First, the evaluation instrument must be developed from the evaluation process. Too often we find that an evaluation instrument is being used which bears little relationship to the actual supervision process. It is extremely important that the evaluation instrument be consistent with the supervision process.

The second assumption is that the evaluation instrument is understood by all teachers and administrators before it is used. This assumption is not important just because of the professional integrity that must be observed. It should be pointed out that orientation to the evaluation instrument is also an orientation to the total evaluation process. This should be the basis for ongoing staff development programs. Much is being said today about in-service for teachers. Development of the evaluation program gives the district an excellent opportunity to conduct an in-service program which would be extremely meaningful and relevant to all concerned.

The third assumption about the evaluation instrument is that checklists and rating scales are useful only if they are used to reflect summarized information gathered from direct observations and discussions. These checklists and rating scales serve little use if they simply reflect a value judgment made by a supervisor or administrator without any agreed upon data or documentation. They should be seen only as summaries of what is taking place. The checklists and rating scales should simply be viewed as tools to facilitate the instructional improvement program. Certainly, they may be used to summarize overall ratings of teachers about total teacher performance over a school year. Once again, these ratings will be meaningful only if they result from systematically gathered information and documentation. It is very easy for the supervisor or administrator to be seen as capricious or arbitrary when checklists and rating scales are used in the absence of information gathered on a regular basis. This point is re-emphasized in the final assumption about the evaluation instrument.

Finally, it is assumed that the use of narrative description is most effective in describing complex activities such as classroom teaching. It has been pointed out several times that classroom teaching is seen as a complex and multi-dimensional activity. Therefore, it is very difficult to reduce such activity to rating scales and checklists. Perhaps there has been too much concern about quantification and converting information to numerical values. Much greater use can be made of detailed narrative descriptions which help to describe the actual activities in the classroom. The analysis of these descriptions by the supervisor and the teacher is essential to improving classroom instruction. It should also be pointed out that numerical ratings become meaningless to administrators who have not had an opportunity to relate the rating to the actual teaching behavior. It is much more informative to the higher level administrator to have comprehensive narrative descriptions which portray strengths and weaknesses of the teacher in the teaching act.

GUIDELINES FOR THE DEVELOPMENT
OF AN EVALUATION PROGRAM

The guidelines which are presented below are believed to be applicable to any district or school. These guidelines have been used by several school districts in developing evaluation programs which do accommodate the different characteristics of the various schools in the district.

The first and perhaps the most important stage in developing an evaluation program is to get general agreement from all concerned with respect to their assumptions about teaching, the role of the supervisor, and the evaluation program.

Professional staff must reach consensus about these assumptions, or the entire evaluation program will be subject to a great deal of internal conflict. Once there is an agreement about the basic assumptions, the administrators and staff members must clarify the roles and responsibilities of all those involved in the evaluation program.

The teachers must understand what their responsibilities are in terms of the evaluation program. They must not only understand their responsibilities but also be willing to accept them. For example, the program may require that teachers document certain activities. If this is the case, the teachers then must take the responsibility to provide the documentation. Further, it might be expected that teachers will be setting goals and targets both for the students and themselves. If so, they must have the goals and targets stated and in writing. These are just examples of the kinds of responsibilities that teachers may have in the overall program.

Supervisors must also agree to carry out the responsibilities of the total evaluation program. If these responsibilities call for them to visit classes on a regular basis and gather objective data about their visitation, this must be done. Further, if as part of their supervisory process, they are expected to conduct pre-observation conferences and post-observation conferences they must carry out this responsibility in good faith. If the supervisors are expected to facilitate the teachers in areas where they currently lack adequate preparation, then it is up to the supervisors to develop the skills necessary to help the teachers. It is essential that the supervisors be seen as professionals who are ready and willing to make a commitment to the responsibilities they have assumed in the evaluation program.

Administrative personnel other than supervisors must also have their responsibilities in the evaluation program clearly delineated. Once this is done they must demonstrate their commitment by conscientiously carrying out their evaluation responsibilities. The evaluation program must be closely related to the district goals and school goals. A school district must have a set of instructional goals which are clearly stated and in writing. In addition, each school in the district must have a statement of goals which is consistent with the district wide goals. These conditions must exist if an evaluation program is to be developed which is congruent with the major thrusts of the school and the district.

Provision should also be made for each individual teacher to set goals regarding his or her instructional expectations for the entire year. These personal goals should be compatible with the local school goals. This practice will help to provide equilibrium within the organization.

It has been pointed out before but should be restated that every attempt should be made to get consensus about important categories for the evaluation instrument. Once these categories have been identified the format for the instrument should be agreed upon. It is too easy to predetermine both categories and format as a result of what other schools and districts are doing. Replicating what others are doing in terms of instrumentation without consideration for local process is in conflict with the philosophy of this entire evaluation program.

Another guideline which has been referred to before is that the supervisory process must be carefully related to the evaluation program. There should be no contradiction in the supervisory procedures and the stated evaluation program. Every effort must be made continually to keep these procedures and the program in concert.

One guideline which is extremely important is that face-to-face meetings of the supervisor and the teacher should be an integral part of all aspects of the evaluation program. These personal discussions should not be relegated to just the formal evaluation activity. They should take place as a matter of course in all aspects of the evaluation program. This starts with the development of the program and continues with orientation and implementation.

There should be no difference in the procedures used in the evaluation program for assessing activities which are not a part of the classroom or teaching responsibility. Agreements should be reached about the responsibilities of the supervisor and the teacher in evaluating outside of classroom activities. Because communities and cultures are so different, it is expected that the responsibilities defined in this aspect of the evaluation program may vary greatly from school to school and district to district.

The evaluation program should focus on the future and use the past as a reference point. Instructional improvement will come only when the supervisor and the teacher are looking ahead and planning new instructional experiences which will overcome weaknesses that have been identified in a collaborative process. Certainly the past activities of the teacher and the supervisors are important in determining new designs. However, too much time and effort can be spent on these past experiences which will have little relevance for the future.

Finally, supervisors, teachers, and administrators should work toward the ultimate goal of the supervision and evaluation program. This goal is instructional improvement through self-evaluation.

EVALUATION INSTRUMENTS

There are a myriad of ways to organize evaluation categories into a school district form. Such a form or instrument should be an outgrowth of the supervisory program. Too often districts change or try to improve their evaluation instruments without relating what they develop to their evaluation assumptions and procedures.

The teachers and administrators in one school district, using the supervisory program described in this book, realized it was necessary to change their evaluation procedures to make them congruent with their supervisory activities. They conducted a series of sessions devoted to identifying the important categories for instructional evaluation. They also agreed on a set of assumptions about the rationale for a good evaluation program. The result was an evaluation instrument that was consistent with their philosophy and administrative procedure.

In addition to the categories for the evaluation instrument, specific responsibilities for the supervisors and teachers were agreed upon. This helped to reinforce the assumption that the primary purpose of the evaluation program was the cooperative improvement of instruction.

We believe the categories and responsibilities identified as being important to this one district might be interesting to those who are considering making a change in their supervision and evaluation programs. Therefore, we have presented the categories and the responsibilities identified as being important to one's district's instructional improvement program. They are:

a. *Student Needs*—The teacher makes an assessment of the students' present skills and knowledge.

> Teacher Responsibility—Describes by what methods the needs were assessed.

> Supervisor Responsibility—Records and discusses the assessment.

b. *Instructional Objectives*—The instructional objectives are started in reference to the characteristics and needs of the learners.

> Teacher Responsibility—Prepares written objective(s) which are necessary for teaching the class.

> Supervisor Responsibility—Identifies and discusses objective(s) in pre and post-observation conferences.

c. *Instructional Strategies*—The teacher's lesson outline shows all learning activities used in the instruction.

> Teacher Responsibility—Provides activities appropriate to the student's learning styles (rate, mode) and abilities.

> Supervisor Responsibility—Observes, records, and discusses the learning activities.

d. *Pupil Performance*—The assessment of pupil performance is made in relation to the stated objectives.

> Teacher Responsibility—Uses on-going assessment techniques and makes modifications and changes in strategies to help students reach the objective(s).

> Supervisor Responsibility—Observes, records, and discusses the assessment techniques.

e. *Student-Teacher Interaction*—Classroom operations include the opportunity for students to interact with each other and with the teacher. Student behavior is supportive of the objective(s).

> Teacher Responsibility—Uses verbal and physical techniques to maximize interaction.

Supervisor Responsibility—Records the frequency of such interaction and presents to the teacher at the post-observation conference.

f. *Knowledge of Subject*—The teacher demonstrates competence of the subject being taught.

Teacher Responsibility—Makes accurate presentation of concepts and facts in subject area(s) of teaching responsibility.

Supervisor Responsibility—Records data regarding the content discussed or used and presents to the teacher at the post-observation conference.

In addition to the evaluation of the teaching-learning activities a school district will have other areas to be included in the evaluation instrument. We would hope that the entire instrument would be the result of a cooperative endeavor among teacher and administrators. Further, we would expect that the rationale for evaluation would be the basis for the development of the instrument.

SUMMARY

Evaluation is the process of gathering information for decision-making. Inherent in this process are a number of important questions. Perhaps the key question to be answered is, "Why are we evaluating?" If the answer does not have to do with improvement, the assumptions and guidelines suggested in this chapter would not be appropriate.

We realize that the pressure is on many school districts to get rid of the ineffective teachers. Certainly, there are ineffective teachers in nearly very district in the country. However, it is the district's responsibility to attempt to help ineffective teachers renew and improve.

The evaluation program can become an important tool for gathering information to provide staff development activities. When teachers have an opportunity to take part in renewal programs aimed at meeting their instructional needs there will be an improvement in the quality of instruction. Information from the evaluation program will also identify those who do not benefit from development and renewal activities. In the few instances where this occurs different alternatives will need to be examined.

DEVELOPMENT AND RENEWAL ACTIVITIES

1. Review the evaluation policies and instruments from several school districts.

2. Analyze the evaluation information from the first activity in order to determine the assumptions that are inherent in the policies and procedures.
3. Compare the assumptions you have identified in activity two with those presented in this chapter.
4. Conduct a brainstorming session with a small group of teachers and administrators to identify and agree upon important evaluation assumptions and procedures.

Chapter 8

Improving Instruction: A Shared Responsibility

When the term supervision is used ,the obvious relationship that comes to mind is the public school supervisor and the classroom teacher. Of course, this is one aspect of supervision that is central to the improvement of instruction. When we begin to analyze supervision in broader terms, and in terms of roles that lend themselves to the improvement of instruction, numerous other relationships appear. Some are more obvious than others.

Many professionals at different levels in a school system are responsible for providing instructional leadership. If a school district is to make a concerted effort toward instructional improvement, it is necessary that those occupying instructional leadership roles function in a cooperative fashion. Teamwork among administrative and supervisory staff and teaching faculties is essential if instructional supervision is to be effective.

Those serving in instructional leadership capacities in school dstricts across the nation include superintendents and assistant superintendents, principals and assistant principals, supervisors, department heads, team leaders, student teaching supervisors, and classroom teachers. Effective supervision is based on the premise that two or more professionals who are concerned with instructional improvement will function cooperatively in attempting to achieve their goals. Teamwork is basic to the supervision process. While roles and responsibilities may differ ,the improvement of instruction should be the common goal of the supervisory team.

The most common teaming relationships utilized in supervision include the supervisor-teacher, principal-teacher, department head-department member. Primary concerns in these relationships may differ. For example, the supervisor may be primarily concerned with methodological improvement while the department head may concentrate on effectiveness in the content area. At the same time, the principal may be most concerned with teacher evaluation. Despite these differing concerns the ultimate purpose in each relationship is to improve instruction.

Supervision need not be restricted to such simple one-to-one relation-ships. The supervisory team can be expanded to include a number of instructional leadership personnel providing feedback to assist teachers and teaching teams in future instructional planning. The supervisory team could include the supervisor, principal, department head, team leader, teachers, or any combination of people in such roles. The supervisory team could consist entirely of a group of teachers collaborating in analytically assessing their instructional effectiveness. The supervisory team consisting entirely of classroom teachers may produce the most effective supervision attainable. A process in which teachers analytically view each other's and their own instruction has a good deal of potential for instructional change.

Although there may be numerous roles for the supervisory process, the basic steps described in previous chapters are still essential (i.e. pre-observation, observation, post-observation). Of course, the differences will appear in such areas as the informality of the conferences, frequency of classroom observations, and the way the supervisory process is used for evaluation.

The purpose of this chapter is to illustrate how the supervision process that has been represented can be adapted to various roles. A point that must be remembered is that these are only a few examples. There are many more possibilities. The process that work best will be unique to each situation after being tried and adapted over a period of time.

THE SUPERVISOR

The role of the supervisor has evolved into one that is specifically concerned with the improvement of instruction. Over the years the role has actually taken on several connotations. Because of the way supervision has often been handled many teachers are often wary of the supervisor.

Of course, all the blame should not be placed on teachers for rejecting the idea of specific supervision designed to make changes in instructional behavior. Supervisors also have intended to reject this notion in favor of a form of ambiguous, non-specific, laissez-faire supervision.

If we start with the assumption that the purpose of supervision is to improve instruction, then analysis of instruction becomes a necessary facet of the supervisory process. The most important function of the supervisor is to guide teachers toward analytical assessment of instruction. In a small district the supervisor may schedule classroom visits periodically with each teacher while in other districts he may make classroom visits by referral from the principal or requests from individual teachers. Still, in larger systems, the supervisor may have the responsibility for training principals, department heads, or team leaders and even individual teachers in the supervisory process. After training those who will be involved in the day-to-day classroom observations, the supervisor can act as a resource person about supervisory process for the instructional and administrative staff. Thus, the supervisor has become the initiator, trainer, facilitator, and resource person while developing a supervisory program.

THE BUILDING PRINCIPAL

Is the principal responsible for the quality of instruction that takes place in his school? If the answer is yes, then the synergetic process of supervision is a tool that the principal can use to help his staff analyze its instructional effectiveness.

A sometimes onerous responsibility that the principal must accept is that of evaluating faculty. In many school districts the evaluation of teachers is haphazardly and poorly done. While the task of evaluating teachers is extremely difficult and often unpleasant, it is necessary to the maintenance of an effective instructional staff. The synergetic process provides a mechanism which can be adapted for evaluative purposes that proves far superior to the traditional checklist procedure for teacher evaluation.

In utilizing the synergetic process for evaluating faculty, the principal and teacher must first agree on the criteria that are the basis for evaluation. Preferably, the teacher objectives will be agreed upon and stated in terms of behavior or performance. The teacher knows the evaluation frame of reference and the principal knows what he is looking for during his observational visits.

In the synergetic approach, it is imperative that the principal visit the classroom and actually observe instruction and the interaction that occurs between pupils and teacher. From this observation an objective record should be developed which can be utilized as a basis for recording what actually occurs in the classroom. This should be done without making value judgments during the observation. The recorded data can then be analyzed cooperatively by the principal and the teacher to determine to what degree the teacher met the objectives that had been previously established. This makes it possible to evaluate teacher instructional effectiveness against agreed upon criteria in an objective manner. The synergetic process provides an effective mechanism by which the principal can meet his concern for both instructional improvement and staff evaluation.

THE DEPARTMENT HEAD

In many schools, although the principal is the designated instructional leader, department heads have been delegated leadership in the instructional process. A close-knit department, where teachers know each other and feel comfortable with each other, can provide an excellent opportunity for the examination of the quality of instruction and the formulation of plans to improve instruction.

In a typical case, the principal may make arrangements to have department heads trained in the supervision process and then let the department heads train and work with their teachers. In this arrangement the principal is the person who provides leadership, direction, resources, and support for his department heads. But the old adage, "You can delegate authority but not responsibility," may hold true here. Although the department heads will be the key leaders in this situation, the ultimate responsibility for the program rests with the principal. Its success or failure will depend, to a great degree, upon his leadership.

In the case of departments utilizing the synergetic process, the factor that the teachers have in common is usually an interest or training in the same subject areas. Many schools have arranged their schedules so that teachers in departments have their planning period together. This provides the organizational time for cooperative planning for improvement.

The department meetings provide an excellent opportunity for teachers to analyze the effectiveness of their methods in relation to subject area content. For example, a social studies department may have purchased some new materials designed for individualized instruction. The department meetings provide excellent opportunities to: discuss which objectives are appropriate with the new material; ways in which the materials might be used effectively; and for planning the kinds of classroom observations that can provide objective feedback to the department.

There are a number of ways for departments to integrate a supervisory process into their everyday teaching. The department head, like the principal and supervisor, may be designated as a key person in the evaluation of faculty. In practically every supervisory role, the synergetic process can be adapted for evaluative purposes. Again, if the supervisory process is being used by department heads for evaluation purposes, the emphasis must be on objective feedback of teaching effectiveness in terms of the teachers' instructional objectives.

THE TEAM LEADER

It would be difficult to think of a more ideal opportunity to examine the quality of classroom instruction than in a team-teaching situation. The team should have jointly planned objectives, strategies, and evaluative techniques. Each member knows what it is he wants the students to learn and the plans that have been made to facilitate the learning. In addition, the team members know the same students. This can be a tremendous asset. Unique characteristics of the classroom situation are known and taken into account by members of the team.

Because they work together each day, the interpersonal relations of the team can relieve much of the anxiety that might normally accompany any type of teacher observation. Of course, this may not be the case, as not all teams work well together. If this is the case, the principal must play an active role in providing leadership and direction in getting the team to function on an open, honest, productive basis where the instruction and learning in the classroom supersede any interteam rivalry. If differences cannot be resolved, the team should probably be reorganized into self-contained classes or into some other appropriate organizational structure.

In a team-teaching situation the best time to plan for supervision is during the planning of the unit. This type of approach allows not only for analysis of instruction but also contributes to thorough planning. For example, a team leader might begin a planning session with the team members by asking, "What is it we want the students to learn as a result of this unit?" In the discussion that follows the teachers will take into account such things as: student entry behavior; affective as well as cognitive learnings; the taxonomic level of learnings; and the characteristics of the students. The important point is that a thorough joint discussion takes place and a consensus is reached as to the overall plan of the unit.

During a second phase of the planning the team leader may provide direction by asking a question similar to, "What methods, materials, and time will we need to implement this unit?" This discussion will focus on the different strengths of team members, availability of materials, and the sequence in which instruction will take place. One must remember that this planning is to provide a general direction for instruction. The strength of a team-teaching situation is the flexibility to depart from scheduled activities and pursue different points as the need arises. However, a good team plans for flexibility by discussing various possibilities so they are better prepared to build on spontaneous occurrences.

As the team discusses which member will have certain assignments, they should make plans for the analysis of instruction. For example, Teacher A might have planned to introduce the lesson to the total group of students. As this is being done another member of the team may be recording the teacher's verbal behavior. A micro-teaching technique may also be used. The point is that if the teacher was introducing the lesson and explaining key points, his being able to later analyze what was said may be helpful in planning future points for discussion with the students. Perhaps the teacher omitted a key point or perhaps there was an announcement over the public address system just as the teacher was giving directions. Maybe everything went fine. Whatever the case, by analyzing the instruction the teacher can evaluate the effectiveness of the lesson.

Another example of team planning for supervision could center around a teacher who plans a discussion on a particular topic. He may ask another member of the team to observe student-student and student-teacher verbal interaction. As the team discusses methods of evaluation plans may be developed to have one member of the team observe student verbal participation or possibly the students' physical activities. Teachers in a team-teaching situation have a unique opportunity to utilize a synergetic process of supervision in improving their instructional effectiveness.

SUPERVISOR OF STUDENT TEACHING

For too long, supervisors of student teaching have felt that they were the key persons in the supervisory process. At the same time the cooperating teacher has been left with little specific training in the analysis of the student teacher's instructional effectiveness. Perhaps, in the area of the student teaching, the role of the cooperating teacher is often misunderstood. Many teachers do help improve the student teachers assigned to them. In other cases the cooperating teacher lacks the training in a process that will allow for systematic observation and analysis of the student teacher's instruction. One function of the college supervisor might be the training in the development of a synergetic process of supervision with the cooperating teachers in the school.

The university supervisor does not abdicate his responsibility for improving the instruction of the student teachers when it is the cooperating teacher who utilizes the supervisory process. Initially, the college supervisor may be responsible for giving training in the processes and skills of analysis. But, as the cooperating teachers and student teachers become skilled and confident in analyzing each other's teaching behavior, the role of the college supervisor becomes much broader.

Providing materials, equipment, support, and giving general leadership and direction to the total effort are examples of the expanded role. This type of role relationship allows the college supervisor to expand his effect upon the student teachers. Rather than periodic evaluation of the student teacher's performance and an occasional visit by the university supervisor, the cooperating teacher and the student teacher can analyze their teaching behavior regularly.

Hopefully, there would be another outcome for the cooperating teacher. If the teacher is analytical about the student teacher's behavior patterns, this may cause the cooperating teacher to become more analytical about his own instruction. When the college supervisor, cooperating teacher, and student teacher work as a team, and systematic instructional planning and analysis is stressed, the quality of the instruction for the students will be improved.

Something should be said about the evaluation of student teachers. Perhaps nothing in the student teaching experience is more difficult than that point when a grade must be given to the student teacher. Many universities are going to a satisfactory, non-satisfactory, grading system, or to a competency-based approach. However, there are many colleges of education where each semester the college supervisor must turn in a letter grade reflecting the quality of the student teacher's work and his potential as a teacher.

Although the task may still be difficult, the college supervisor, the cooperating teacher, and the student teacher can arrive at a more accurate and fair assessment of the student teacher if a careful analysis of the student teacher's instruction has taken place. Student teaching is a time when the student teacher attempts to improve his instructional effectiveness. A record compiled by utilizing a cooperative process of supervision can provide an accurate account of the student teacher's performance.

Nowhere is the application of the word "synergetic" more important than in student teaching. In order for the experience to be rewarding for everyone involved, an open, honest, helpful relationship must exist. If it does not, the college supervisor must make the establishment of such a relationship his highest priority.

SUMMARY

There are many different organizational arrangements in schools and other educational agencies. Within each organization roles and responsibilities are delineated. Supervision and evaluation responsibilities vary depending on the role delineation. The philosophy of the people in the organization will shape the processes which make up the instructional improvement program. Therefore, the approach to change and improvement will be the result of the organizational structure, role and responsibility delineation ,and underlying philosophy of the staff.

Whatever the arrangements, attempts to improve instruction will have a greater chance to succeed when it is a cooperative endeavor. Independent action should not be considered as being non-productive. Teachers, administrators, department heads, and university supervisors, can all achieve certain goals independent of one another. When they work together to analyze and improve instruction the chances are very good that significant contributions to the instructional program will be made.

DEVELOPMENT AND RENEWAL ACTIVITIES

1. Review the organizational structure and administrative policies of a school district as they relate to supervision and evaluation.
2. Talk with several members of the school staff who have been designated as instructional leaders. Try to determine how they perceive their role and responsibility in the supervision and evaluation program.
3. Conduct an instructional needs assessment for a school. Identify the instructional improvement needs that teachers perceive need attention. Identify the instructional support given by administrators, supervisors, department heads, and other members of the administrative and support system. Analyze and compare your findings to determine the instructional gaps (needs).
4. Using the needs identified in activity three, outline a staff development program for the teachers, administrators, and support staff. By using the rationale that development and renewal are necessary for personnel at all levels of the organization, you will be able to include most of the staff in your plan.